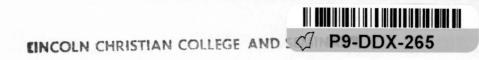

Leadership
Is the Key

BOOKS IN THE LEADERSHIP INSIGHT SERIES

LEADERSHIP INSIGHT SERIES
LEADERSHIP INSIGHT SERIES
LEADERSHIP INSIGHT SERIES

Leadership Is the Key

Unlocking Your Effectiveness in Ministry

HERB MILLER, EDITOR

A moment of insight is worth a lifetime of experience

HERB MILLER

Abingdon Press
Nashville

LEADERSHIP IS THE KEY:
UNLOCKING YOUR EFFECTIVENESS IN MINISTRY

Library of Congress Cataloging-in-Publication Data

Miller, Herb.
    Leadership is the key: unlocking your effectiveness in ministry/
Herb Miller.
        p.   cm.—(Leadership insight series)
    Includes bibliographical references.
    ISBN 0-687-01375-5 (pbk.: alk. paper)
    1. Christian leadership.   I. Series.
BV652.1.M538   1997
253—DC21   96-51887

97 98 99 00 01 02 03 04 05 06—10 9 8 7 6 5 4 3 2 1

MANUFACTURED IN THE UNITED STATES OF AMERICA

To the clergy,
lay staff,
and congregations
who have invited me
into their lives

CONTENTS

Contents

PREFACE

A survey asked regional leaders in several denominations across the United States what their congregations needed most from pastors. One word surfaced many times: *leadership*. Tons of books and magazine articles on the importance of leadership have rolled off religious and business presses in recent years. Why does this crucial quality still seem AWOL?

For at least four major reasons, giving effective church leadership is much more difficult these days than it used to be. First, between 40 and 70 percent of every congregation's members grew up in or transferred their membership from a congregation in another denomination. This ecclesiastical homogenization process, which began during the 1960s, replaces a previous era in which less than 10 percent of any congregation's members had crossed denominational lines. (In the 1920s, many people called the marital union of a Presbyterian and a Methodist a mixed marriage.) People in different denominations differ in their definition of good leadership. They bring these differences into their new church homes and articulate them in meetings and hallway buzz groups. Most pastors are leading churches whose members want to go in several directions simultaneously.

Second, congregations within the same denominational family differ greatly from one another in regard to their chief operating focus. What happens when a parishioner transfers from a congregation with a different focus? He or she will spend the next several years either (a) rejoicing in "how much better it is here," or (b) consciously or unconsciously trying to change the adopted congregation into the type with which she or he is more comfortable.

Third, the new societal ideal of pluralism—born in the 1960s—began affirming the need to respect the individualism expressed in minority opinion. This replaced the previous ideal—officially born in 1776—that expected minority viewpoints to quietly acquiesce to majority votes. People bring to their congregations a set of expectations as diverse as heat-induced explosions in a paint store. When it appears in congregations, the desire to make decisions by majority vote while staying concerned about minority opinion makes every kind of church leadership role at least five times more complicated.

The fourth reason congregations often clamor for leadership is that they have had painful experiences with ministerial and lay staff leaders who have rowed their churches' boats in directions the congregations did not want to go. Not everyone who complains about lack of leadership really means that their leaders are not leading. What some mean is that their leadership is different from what they think the congregation or organization needs.

The information in this volume of the *Leadership Insight Series* cannot reverse history. It therefore concentrates on providing tools and insights for clergy, lay staff, and lay leaders who want to strengthen their ability to make decisions that increase their personal sense of meaning and satisfaction while simultaneously increasing the effectiveness of their congregation or organization's mission and ministry.

—Herb Miller, Lubbock, Texas

INTRODUCTION

Community Church fired John. Looking back on this painful experience five years later, John called it a mismatch. But he still did not understand what happened. The parishioners in his next congregation said he was the best pastor they had ever had. So he wrote off the bad experience as a black hole and thought of it less and less.

Joy was unhappy as a part-time youth director. In her repeated attempts at enlarging the youth groups, she felt as if she were trying to build a tuna sandwich without bread. After two frustrating years, the senior pastor asked her to change positions.

"I think you would be perfect as our part-time membership care coordinator," he said. Two years later, he invited her to go full time in that role.

"The job is expanding, and no one can do it as well as you," he said.

The short explanation for the previous illustrations is that church leaders are different from one another. Their "differentness" is the prime determiner of their effectiveness in specific congregations and ministry roles. Beneath that simple explanation, however, many questions clamor for a longer answer:

- What causes the differentness?
- How can clergy and lay staff identify their differentness and predict whether they would fit into a particular congregation or ministry role?

- If their differentness ill fits their ministry position, can leaders alter themselves enough to fit the situation? If so, how?
- Can call committees and personnel committees find ways to identify differentness in advance?
- How can senior pastors identify ministry ability patterns in emerging leaders so as to correctly match people with board and committee positions?

Accurately answering such questions requires more than the single-cause explanations of differentness often heard in church hallway conversations. The inner self is a complex combination of numerous deeply held values, priorities, and ideals of conduct. Carl Jung called this true inner self the *anima,* contrasting it in his analytic psychology with the individual's role in life (external *persona*). Since contemporary writers use *anima* in a quite different way from Jung's original meaning, *intrinsic* is a more understandable term. The dictionary defines *intrinsic* as "belonging to the inmost constitution or essential nature of a thing." (*Extrinsic,* by contrast, means "from without, on the outside.")

Whatever we call this true inner self, its complex features are the hidden determinants of whether clergy, staff, and lay leaders fit the needs of a particular congregation or ministry role. Church leaders who do not genuinely enjoy teenagers, for example, can energetically attempt youth leadership roles but seldom excel at them. Sending such leaders to training events that provide extrinsic information about their role is not enough.

Each church leader's intrinsic nature is like a ten-layer cake that contains ten kinds of inner values or motivations. Each of these ten intrinsic drive patterns helps to determine whether a leader will excel in a particular congregation or ministry role. Taken together, these ten intrinsic characteristics make up the individual's "ministry abilities pattern." These ten intrinsic components that underlie every clergy and church staff leader's extrinsic persona may not be the only ones, but they are basic ones. Church leaders are effective to the extent that these ten intrinsic characteristics fit the needs of the congregation or church organization they serve.

Some of these ten intrinsic characteristics are deeply rooted in the individual's personality; thus, they are not easily changed. People can, however, modify some of these intrinsic qualities in order to increase their effectiveness in a particular ministry role. For example, many pastors are intrinsically introverts rather than extroverts (introverts draw emotional energy from being alone rather than from being with others). Yet, many introverted pastors are excellent leaders. They have learned how to be extroverted for brief periods when that behavior is essential, such as on Sunday mornings.

Some would argue against the possibility that people can make genuine, lasting changes in their intrinsic ministry abilities pattern. The evidence does not support that fatalistic viewpoint. Every Christian who experiences a deep and lasting conversion to Jesus Christ knows that intrinsic personality characteristics can change, sometimes instantly. Clergy and staff experience less dramatic kinds of intrinsic conversion throughout a lifetime of ministry. One pastor named a national event he attended as the birthday of his conviction regarding the importance of evangelistic outreach. Many leaders report that education in the form of books, magazines, and personal conversations with respected mentors changed one or more of their intrinsic values. Personal experience, especially during the first decade of church leadership roles, often changes intrinsic characteristics enough to permanently modify a ministry abilities pattern.

As church leaders become more consciously aware of their hidden leadership effectiveness determinants, they are more likely to choose ministry roles in which they excel. As they become more consciously aware of their inner drive mix, they become more productive and satisfied, finding a greater sense of meaning and purpose in their Christian calling. As they become more consciously aware of their intrinsic ministry abilities pattern, they can decide whether they should try to alter those intrinsic characteristics that do not fit with their present congregation or ministry role.

In one "Calvin and Hobbes" comic strip, Calvin, sitting in a little red wagon, tells Hobbes, who is pushing the wagon, that ignorance is bliss. As the cartoon frames unfold, Calvin says that knowing things causes you to see problems everywhere. If, however, you are willfully stupid, you can keep doing things the same way. The two characters see that their little red wagon is headed for a cliff, but they keep on going. In the final frame, they are lying at the bottom of the cliff. Hobbes says that he is not sure he can stand this much bliss.

People who have done time in a ministry role mismatched with their intrinsic ministry abilities pattern usually echo those sentiments. Trying to stick a smiley face on the pain, they may call it a "learning experience." Privately, however, they would prefer to gain their insights some other way. This book addresses people's need to learn about their ministry abilities patterns by illustrating (a) the numerous options from which clergy and staff consciously and unconsciously select the shape of ten inner drives that underlie their leadership persona, (b) some results of those choices with regard to leadership effectiveness, and (c) how to change to more appropriate options if those new directions seem desirable and possible.

Each clergy and lay staff member plays a visible, *extrinsic* tune with a hidden, *intrinsic* instrument. Will the visible, extrinsic song be a platform for meaning and satisfaction or a prison of frustration and disharmony? That depends on whether the hidden, intrinsic ministry abilities pattern fits (or whether we can sufficiently change it to fit) the congregation or ministry role in which we serve. This makes discovering the hidden determinants of leadership strength much more than a means of increasing congregational or organizational effectiveness. Such knowledge can immeasurably increase, not just the leader's ability to sing, but how much the leader enjoys his or her life song.

CHAPTER 1

IS YOUR FUTURE IN YOUR PAST?

Most church members agree that effective clergy and staff possess a combination of character, competence, compassion, experience, personality, faithfulness, and productivity. But these attributes do not tell the whole story. A larger picture includes the directions in which the staff member focuses those qualities. That leadership direction, or inner motivation construct, can fit quite well in one congregation or organization but produce dismal failure in another.

Every clergy and staff member who links up with a congregation or an organization comes equipped with a ministry model ideal. Invisible in personnel committee and call committee interviews (or the early months of ministry in denominations with appointive systems), the leader's ministry model ideal gradually begins looking like a blessing or a curse over the next two or three years. If the leader's ministry model ideal fits with the ideal image held by most of the people in the congregation or group, a happy marriage is beginning. If these two unstated ministry model ideals do not match, grounds for divorce are forming.

Leaders who want to more effectively select the congregations and ministry roles in which they serve should ask themselves, *Which ministry model did I choose during college, seminary, or the early years of my ministry experience as the ideal image of effectiveness?* The committees that select people for church positions increase their effectiveness to the degree that they uncover the answer to that question prior to the marriage. A leader's ministry model ideal—an invisible, intrinsic characteristic that underlies and influences the way he or she does every visible, extrinsic ministry position—is one of ten hidden determinants of his or her leadership strength.

Fifteen Ministry Model Ideals

The child is parent of the adult. That adage, persuasively argued in many self-help books, tells us that childhood feeling and thinking patterns last a lifetime. The principle applies in a slightly revised translation among church leaders: I am what I was in my late teens, as a new adult Christian, or during my first years of salaried Christian service—with a little more mileage on the odometer. Early in their church experiences, all clergy and staff consciously or unconsciously (usually a mixture of both) choose a ministry model ideal. That model leaves its fingerprints on the leader and the persons led throughout a lifetime of Christian service in a variety of situations and circumstances.

Ministry model ideals come in at least fifteen forms. Most leaders who read the list below will identify in themselves a primary model and two or three secondary models. This combination makes a major contribution to the shape of their ministry abilities pattern.

1. The sociological model. After emerging as an important science and rising to curriculum prominence in some seminaries during the 1950s, sociology became the polar star of many seminary graduates as they settled into a lifetime of parish ministry. For example, a pastor who grew up in a large metropolitan church accepted a congregational call in a western Kansas town, population two thousand. He became very effective there, priding himself on understanding the sociological patterns and needs of people in this church and community.

Another graduate of the same seminary experienced opposite results. His keen sociological observation skills did not make the same kind of transition from analysis to application. He evaluated the culture in his adopted community and found it lacking sophistication at numerous points. Basing his prophetic sermons on that analysis, he battered people with a stream of graceless judgments that they accurately assessed as rejection. Soon, they rejected him. His new role in the denomination's national department that helped middle judicatories select new church sites fit his ministry model ideal perfectly. He served there for two decades and became a highly respected denominational leader.

2. The psychological model. Pastoral psychology achieved prominence as a valuable helping skill following World War II. By the early 1960s, many seminaries had developed departments to teach this new science. During that period, which also saw rapidly increasing numbers of community mental health centers across the country, many pastors chose pastoral care as their ministry model ideal.

Clergy who adopted this model experienced a variety of end results. One pastor, for example, integrated this specialized skill into a broad range of other abilities. While recognized as "someone you can talk to," he also had strong administrative, evangelism, preaching, and biblical teaching abilities. He limited his counseling efforts to not more than three sessions per person and referred people with special or long-term needs to other community professionals.

Another pastor took a different road. His first church was located in a community with no psychiatric or psychological services. Soon, he had every day from 1:00 P.M. to 6:00 P.M. booked full of counseling appointments. Ninety percent of these clients were from outside the congregation. He felt great personal satisfaction in helping people, but his ministry speciality became a time captivity. Although he maintained a strong reputation for faithful, caring hospital visitation, his counseling ability became a liability to other parts of his pastoral role. He had no time left for anything else. Eventually, he accepted a full-time position in a local medical center. (A friend of his took a variation of this road and became a full-time counselor on the staff of a large congregation.)

During their first few years of postseminary experience, pastors unconsciously or consciously become chaplains or apostles. Chaplains care about people one at a time, assuming that healthy people will take care of leading the congregation. Apostles integrate counseling abilities into a skill quiver containing several other arrows, assuming that a pastor must both care about individuals and give leadership oversight to the congregation. Clergy are more likely to become chaplains if (a) they were educated during the 1960s, (b) they majored in pastoral care in seminary, (c) they grew up in a small town, (d) their first postseminary church was small, (e) their first postseminary church was small-town or rural, (f) they have an above average need for love and affirmation, (g) their introverted personality pattern makes them more comfortable talking with individuals than with groups, (h) they get more satisfaction from making a difference by helping individuals than from making a difference by helping groups of people, or (i) their initial sense of "call" to ministry came from a generalized desire to spend their life in a service vocation.

3. The scholarship model. This can take a variety of forms that look different from each other but grow from the same root. Some clergy who adopt this model invest in the several additional years of academic study necessary to become seminary professors—a ministry role in which transmitting ideas is the primary job. Other clergy spend a lifetime as local pastors who focus on New Testament Greek, biblical archaeology (including numerous "digs" in the Holy Land), or some other academic speciality. For some such clergy, their academic pursuit becomes a hobby that provides a healthy diversion from the intensity of church leadership roles. The parishioners of other such clergy begin to feel that the academic speciality, instead of assisting with the pastor's ministry, has become the ministry.

Pastors do not become effective without books and study. But what happens if a fascination with ideas significantly outdistances their enjoyment in working with people? Spending time with books can become an unconscious substitution for several other essential parts of congregational ministry. When that happens, (a) pastors have difficulty seeing the substitution because their academic hobby feels so important to their ministry, (b) lay leaders in their congregations will see the ministry elements being neglected but not know how to suggest that the pastor take corrective action, and (c) the pastor-people relationships begin a slow trip toward voluntary or involuntary termination.

By contrast, many local pastors recognize and deal with this "academic idolatry temptation" in their first five years out of seminary. During these transition-to-the-real-world years, they recognize the big differences between preparation for the parish and actually serving in the parish. Seminary life rewards a scholastic orientation requiring much time spent alone; congregations reward an interpersonal, community orientation requiring much time spent with people and groups. Seminaries emphasize the importance of intellectualizing, knowing that this lays a solid conceptual base for a lifetime of service; congregations emphasize the practical skills needed for getting things done.

Pastors who successfully negotiate the rapids of this transition from seminary to congregation retain their academic focus. But they use it as a tool for ministry rather than letting it divert them from ministry. They recognize and deal with the temptation to lock in on a target that was important in seminary but matters far less to people in congregations. They recognize that learned people show the greatest ignorance when they substitute the possession of knowledge for the application of knowledge. They understand that rational thinking, taken in large doses without spiritual application, is idolatry to the self.

A few church leaders, of course, find their niche in an academic ministry such as teaching or a denominational staff role. In those jobs, transmitting effective ideas to the leaders of congregations is of paramount importance. Therefore, the scholarship model is both effective for ministry and personally fulfilling.

4. The administrative model. Leaders who adopt this model enjoy church roles similar to those of corporate executives. They derive satisfaction from managing a productive and effective organization. People with this ministry model ideal are often effective as business managers in large congregations or Christian organizations. Some senior pastors of large churches excel in their ministry because this is their primary mental model. Staff members who lead specialized ministry departments in large congregations also benefit from this kind of focus.

5. The Holy Spirit model. In denominations such as the Assemblies of God, clergy seldom attain professional upward mobility without a strong emphasis on miracles, physical healing, spiritual gifts (including speaking in tongues), and "Spirit-filled" worship services. Spiritual edification through a sense of God's presence and his willingness to set aside the cause-and-effect laws of science and biology are the central ministry focus.

By contrast, few leaders in mainline denominations are blessed with professional advancement if they enthusiastically espouse all of these beliefs and practices. They expect God to occasionally but not often act outside the laws of nature. Their convictions regarding the third person of the Trinity tend toward belief in more intellectualized influences through creative urges and enhanced rational thinking; they far less frequently express belief in God's direct intervention in human reality. They understand God more as a creator than as a mechanic who frequently steps in to fix what is broken.

Clergy and church staff are effective in their congregations and ministry positions to the extent that these intrinsic beliefs fit with those of the people they serve. A significant mismatch of this ministry model ideal between staff person and congregation, unlike some other kinds of mismatches, generates quick and intense conflict. Church people seem particularly unforgiving when other Christians express differences of opinion regarding how God can behave.

6. The teaching model. People who adopt this ministry model ideal draw energy from and often excel at teaching biblical information or ministry skills. Many effective associate pastors in large congregations (including pastors whose major strengths are with youth, Christian education, and music) work from this ministry orientation base. Clergy associates and lay staff may seldom or never have congregational visibility through preaching. Yet they can develop strong leadership reputations from their strength in teaching.

By contrast, of course, someone whose ministry position is primarily a teaching role becomes both unhappy and unsuccessful if he or she is motivated by a fellowship model or a preaching model.

7. The fellowship model. People who adopt this ministry model bring a fun-loving nature to their Christian service. Usually warm and caring when relating to individuals, a family reunion atmosphere is their central goal in group relationships. Many effective youth leaders operate from this ideal. Their contagious joy attracts followers, some of whom are surprised that deeply religious people can have a good time.

A small percentage of pastors and associate pastors with this orientation get opposite results: If it is their only focus, their congregations or organizations become a continuous party where not much else happens. Some of the participants begin to feel that they need an occasional steak to supplement all this cotton candy.

If, however, the fellowship ideal is accompanied by one of two or three other foci—such as preaching and administration—the combination creates an effective senior pastor leadership mix. Similar combinations work well in other church roles. Some of the most effective adult class teachers, for example, are motivated by the twin ideals of teaching and fellowship.

8. The preaching model. Clergy who adopt this ministry ideal often but not always gain satisfaction from worship leadership in general. Sometimes, their focus is so word-oriented that they take little or no interest in other parts of the service, such as music. Other such pastors enjoy every aspect of preparing for and leading worship, funeral services, weddings, and other public events. Senior pastors in large churches, many of whom begin to feel like one-person speaking factories, often possess this ministry model ideal. That internal drive allows them to keep trudging ahead through endless weeks in which they average twenty or more hours in speaking preparation.

Some of the unhappiest clergy are motivated by the preaching model ideal but serve as associate pastors who preach four to six times each year. They have two choices if they want to escape what feels like a prison: (1) Seek a solo pastor or senior pastor position. (2) Redirect their preaching model urges by throwing their energies into teaching an adult Sunday school class.

9. The social action model. People who adopt this ministry ideal come in one of two forms, or a mixture of both. Some find joy in helping needy people with food, clothing, housing, and so forth. Their orientation is selfless service, which can manifest itself in setting up soup kitchens or similar endeavors. Other people with this ministry ideal take a prophetic stance. They write letters to the editor, speak out on public issues from the pulpit, and lobby elected officials. A few people combine service with prophecy. They help hurting people, but they also speak out in ways that they hope will improve the system that creates hurting people.

One such service-prophetic pastor has for two decades modeled leadership excellence in a downtown Detroit church situated in a formerly middle-class neighborhood now dominated by crime, drugs, poverty, and the homeless. The church has invented and is housing fourteen nonprofit organizations to deal with various human needs. The pastor is well known among state legislators, and regional denominational structures seek his advice on many issues.

Would that ministry model work in a western Nebraska town of two thousand? Only if the pastor stayed ten years and patiently developed a reputation as "the community's pastor." Many small churches and small towns hear irascible prophets as gladly as fingernails scratching a blackboard. Pushing such pastors away into some distant wilderness seems better than extended listening.

10. The missions model. One individual who is motivated by this model is a missionary to the Wa people in northern Thailand. Growing up as a Thai missionary's son surely influenced his decision to become a missionary himself. However, not all missionaries' children adopt the missions model ideal. Factors other than personal experience determine this selection.

Not everyone with this orientation serves in another country. Some pastors and lay leaders see missions as their congregation's primary calling. Women's organizations are especially likely to contain several leaders for whom this is the primary agenda item. Some persons motivated by the missions model judge adults who do not share their focus as sadly lacking in Christian virtue. This clash of ministry model ideals explains why participation in church women's organizations has diminished by one-third to two-thirds during the past three decades. Virtually all church women and many of the men held this ideal in the 1880s. Far fewer espoused it in the 1950s. Now, a very small percentage see it as the main focus.

11. The fund-raising model. We saw many examples of this kind of pastor during the 1950s. Soldiers returning from World War II flooded the churches with their presence and progeny. Constructing Christian education space and larger sanctuaries became a necessity. This building boom had twin driveshafts: the highest birth rate in history and increasing church attendance. In 1957 and 1959, 49 percent of Americans attended worship on a typical weekend. (Those all-time highs fell quickly back to about 40 percent in the 1970s.)

Some pastors who excelled at capital fund campaigns left a forty-year trail of buildings in several communities. Congregations that needed a new building called (or the bishop appointed) such individuals as pastors. In some cases, those pastors created a building vision soon after they arrived, either because they unlocked the congregation's repressed need for more space or because this was the ministry they knew best how to do.

Other clergy with this ministry ideal dramatically increase their members' per capita giving level to the operating budget in every church they pastor. Because they understand the invisible stewardship principles that unlock the motivations that unlock pocketbooks, piles of money appear in churches previously held hostage by the poverty syndrome. Some such clergy gravitate to leadership roles in their denominations' stewardship departments or development offices in retirement homes. Others become college presidents, a role in which discomfort with asking people for money automatically shortens one's occupancy.

12. The evangelism model. This ministry model, prevalent during the 1930s, was rare by the 1970s. Two decades of full pews following World War II caused many mainline clergy to think evangelism endeavors unnecessary. Others decided that new members are always a secondary by-product of doing other church programs well, and hence irrelevant to their leadership effectiveness. Still others, a bit embarrassed by their membership growth success, started saying to each other "Let's not play the numbers game." Disdain for this ministry model ideal peaked in the mid-1960s. Some mainline denominations voted in their national meetings to stop planting any new churches as a matter of principle.

Beginning in the 1980s and continuing to the present, a slightly higher percentage of young pastors began exhibiting an evangelism ministry model ideal. Some of them are entrepreneurial in personality, a trait often seen in second-career pastors who spent the first part of their lives in businesses and corporations. Other, younger pastors, arrive at their evangelism convictions from a purely theological orientation or from college conversion experiences through Campus Crusade or other such organizations. A few pastors caught this vision because their first service out of seminary was in a new church. At a national meeting, for example, evangelism leaders from several denominations discovered that each of them had planted a new church thirty years ago.

A growing number of denominational leaders now advocate the evangelism ideal, their conviction fueled by a combination of theological reflection, declining membership, and the sound of money not hitting the national missions collection plate. As mainline denominations "bottom out" their membership slides around the year 2020, many of their top pastors will carry the evangelism model ideal into the rebuilding stage.

13. The music model. For the individual motivated by this model, relating people to God through singing and worshiping is the central ministry focus. Some clergy live out this trait with a lifetime of choir participation or solo worship specials. A few clergy and many laypersons enter full-time or part-time church music leadership positions.

The most frustrated people in this group are young pastors with some music training and a great deal of natural talent. They find themselves chained to a much older choir director or organist who was trained during the 1940s or the 1950s in classical church music. Some musicians never grow beyond their training experience. They do not understand the changed worship music preferences of younger adults; or if they do, they abhor them as inferior. Such musicians see many of their post-college adults joining evangelical denominations that feed their hunger for a broader range of worship music. Yet choir directors of this "arrested development" type do not have a clue as to why. In defense, such musicians often say, "They just don't understand good music"—not realizing that they are stating their own birthdate more clearly than their music credentials.

14. The small-group model. Sometimes called "ring leaders," clergy who adopt this ministry model ideal focus on developing personal faith and congregational vitality through prayer, Bible study, and sharing groups. A Portland, Oregon, pastor of this type grew a church to 6,000 in average worship attendance. More than 4,200 of the members meet weekly in small groups. Another such pastor grew a small-town, southeastern Ohio church from 200 to more than 2,000 in average worship attendance in fifteen years. More than 50 percent of the members attend weekly small group sessions.

Clergy do not as often adopt this ministry model ideal in seminary as in subsequent years. Usually, they catch the vision by attending a conference or through a clergy colleague who understands the principles of small group development and oversight. A combination of motivations in which the secondary orientations of administration and preaching reinforce the small group ministry model ideal can create a strong leadership package for building churches of this type.

Clergy who are strongly motivated by the small group drive will feel unhappy and unproductive in circumstances where they cannot live out their convictions. Many laypersons who experienced the warm sense of community and spiritual growth of small group participation feel eternally uncomfortable in other kinds of churches.

15. The spiritual guide model. Clergy and lay staff who are motivated from this inner drive make spirituality the hub of their ministry wheel. Some people choose this path because mysticism is their natural personality bent. Other people concentrate on spiritual growth because a personal crisis turns them toward God and prayer. Having drunk this life-changing water, they energetically offer it to others. The rising tide of interest in "spiritual direction" in recent years has also attracted some church leaders to this focus.

However they caught this ideal, these Christians feel that their primary calling is not church work but helping people connect with God and grow in that relationship. Among mainline denominations especially, a spirituality focus helps to balance the vacuousness of faith experience to which several decades of overemphasis on rational thinking has led (a result observed several times throughout Christian history). Involving both rational thinking and emotional feeling, but transcending both, a spiritual guide focus points people toward God with methods that the Christian mystics have used throughout the ages.

Only a few senior pastors adopt this ministry model, which until the past fifteen years was more prevalent among Roman Catholics than Protestants. The spiritual guide model is more often observed among lay staff and associate pastors. By making this their ministry speciality, they develop a positive self-identity that sets them apart from other church leaders.

The unhappiest of such leaders are trapped in jobs where they must spend 90 percent of their ministry time shepherding administrative details and paperwork. Church members and other kinds of leaders will see those organizational tasks as important, necessary church work; spiritual guide type pastors will see administrative tasks as meaningless trivia that leave them no time to do the work of the church.

Senior pastors who adopt this model move in one of two directions: (a) they gather one or several staff who excel in handling the details of administrative work, delegating to them both leadership authority and responsibility, or (b) they cocoon themselves into a spiritual guide focus while their congregation's membership and financial strength slides downhill over a period of several years. Laypeople find senior pastors who take the latter road (unbalanced with administrative detail support) easy to criticize and discharge. Many church members will affirm their deep spirituality, but ultimately, involuntary termination occurs. The attendance and finances eventually fall so low that church board members will say, "The pastor is a fine person of God, but we have no choice."

The happiest of spiritual guide leaders serve in ministry roles where their focus complements or is the central goal of their job description. People who are motivated by the spiritual guide model may be happy and effective as associate pastors in charge of membership care, national staff who have large blocks of discretionary time, and teachers in "spiritual director" positions.

Which Model Is Best?

Did Jesus use one of the fifteen ministry model ideals listed earlier in this chapter? Yes and no. *Teacher* is the most frequent label the Gospel writers give Jesus. Several dozen times we read, "And he taught them, saying . . . " Yet a thorough search of the written records reveals other activities. Jesus repeatedly engaged in eight behaviors: (1) he prayed; (2) he studied; (3) he taught; (4) he preached; (5) he traveled; (6) he befriended people; (7) he healed people physically; (8) he healed people mentally and emotionally.

Knowing Jesus' ministry model does not automatically give us our model. We are not God and cannot expect to do everything he did the way he did it. We can, however, draw one important insight from Jesus' behavior. He used the ministry model that fit the ministry need of each moment; he did not try to force one model onto all situations. Jesus' present-day disciples can increase their leadership effectiveness by more frequently applying his principle of accurate selectivity—consciously sensing and using a ministry model that fits their congregation or position. An old axiom says that nothing is worse than a good idea if it is the only idea you have. Something is worse, however: Having a good idea that is not the idea you need in this congregation or ministry role.

How can you find out which model is needed? Prayer, Bible study, consciousness of your ministry model predispositions, and rational thinking are good starting points. Careful listening is an especially useful tool. Find out what worked and did not work for persons who preceded you. Pastors, for example, can benefit from asking a call committee questions such as the following: What did your last two pastors do extremely well? What gaps did you notice in their ministries? What programs did they start that you would not want to give up? What activities did they start that most of the members would not mind letting go?

Few pastors and staff members will feel God leading them to clone their predecessor's past. Yet knowing what ministry models worked and did not work is priceless. Unknowingly or knowingly rejecting some cherished part of the past comes across as rejection of your congregation's or organization's basic purpose for existence. Staff who build that kind of barrier can seldom climb over it.

A farmer showed up at a county fair with a pumpkin exactly the shape of a two-gallon jug. Someone asked how he did it. He said, "I put the pumpkin vine into the glass jug when the pumpkin was tiny. It expanded to fit the jug but no further." To a great extent, every staff member's ministry model ideal is already formed. Factors over which he or she exerted little conscious control have shaped it. His or her future *is* in the past. However, the first pages of the Bible say that people are not pumpkins; they are free to choose how they think and react.

The last pages of the New Testament add an even more important possibility to that freedom: "Behold, I make all things new" (Rev. 21:5). People can make choices. People can replace previous choices with new choices. People can let God's spirit help them reshape their choices. Our future is in our past only to the extent that we settle for being pumpkin people rather than children of God.

CHAPTER 2

WHICH JESUS DO YOU FOLLOW?

On the southwest corner of the courthouse square in a small Kansas town, three churches occupy three corners of the intersection. Each pastor posts the next Sunday's sermon title on a sign in front of the church. One Monday morning the Presbyterian pastor's title said, "The Kingdom of God." Later that morning, the Methodist pastor put up his sermon title: "Enter the Kingdom Here." That afternoon, the Baptist pastor, whose church was between the other two, posted his title: "Main Entrance."

That kind of interchange among clergy from different denominations—which happened early in the twentieth century—seldom occurs today. The sharp doctrinal distinctions that once marked the boundaries between denominations are less noticeable now. The fistfights that sometimes broke out between zealous church members on Saturday afternoons in small towns across the South are unheard of in our day. This does not mean, however, that differing theological winds no longer blow. The arguments have relocated. Newspapers report wrangling debates from the floor of regional and national denominational meetings. The religious wars have come indoors. Instead of criticizing other denominations, leaders *within* each denomination hotly debate theological issues related to proper Christian conduct, church polity, and a variety of other matters.

What causes such sharp differences of opinion among sincere Christian people? Do we not all read the same Bible? Do we not all follow the same Christ? Do we not all attempt to live by his teachings? If so, how do we arrive at such differing conclusions? The answer lies in the theological selectivity we use when we study Jesus' teachings. According to the four Gospel writers' records, Jesus used twenty different themes as he told people how to connect with God and live a meaningful life. Without consciously intending to, we pick from Jesus' twenty themes the ones that seem the most important to us and see the others as less significant. Many of the heated arguments within denominations are power and control issues disguised as theological convictions. Many of the genuinely theological differences stem from sincere people adopting different lists from among the twenty topics Jesus covered.

Jesus' Big Idea

Biblical scholars at every point on the theological compass agree on Jesus' central message. He focused on the kingdom of God. He used that three-word phrase more than 110 times in the New Testament: *kingdom of God*. Across the centuries, however, definitions and explanations of that central term have achieved far less consensus among scholars. Hundreds of books have attempted to explain it, through the use of various metaphors and analogies. Each of these, at different moments in history, has made a contribution to Christian thinking about Jesus' term, kingdom of God.

Many scholars, however, recognize the indefinable nature of Jesus' term. The kingdom of God describes a phenomenon that lies mostly outside the range of human explanation. Therefore, using a metaphor (a figure of speech that denotes likeness between one kind of object or idea and another completely different object or idea) is the only way we can discuss the kingdom of God.

One kingdom metaphor that makes sense to many contemporary laypersons is "new level of consciousness." Every human being experiences shifts in level of consciousness. Consider these examples:

- Do you remember the first time you fell in love? The day that happened, you became an entirely different person. Everything changed.

Your thinking and behavior suddenly came under the control of a whole new perspective. You looked at the world through a new mental window. You had entered a new "level of consciousness."

- Anger is another level of consciousness that changes your perspective. During the moments when you are caught in the grip of anger, your thinking and behavior temporarily shift to different gears. You become a different person than you were before.

- Fear is another level of consciousness. What was the most frightening situation you ever experienced? During that time, was your thinking about what is important and what is unimportant radically altered? You were still the same person—yet you were not the same person. All your motives, aspirations, and priorities were momentarily reshuffled.

- Depression or "the blues" is yet another level of consciousness. When you are in the grip of that deadening mood, you look at the world through negative-colored glasses. Your "apperceptive set" has been temporarily restructured.

What was Jesus asking Peter to do that day at the seashore when he said, "Follow me"? What was he asking Matthew to do that day at the tax office in Capernaum when he said, "Follow me"? He was inviting both of them to enter a new level of consciousness that would change their perspectives, priorities, and behaviors.

That happens to every person who experiences Christian conversion. With some people, this comes instantly. With others, the process is slower. But every type of conversion has a beginning point. At a particular moment in time, the person enters a new level of consciousness in which God and his truths become a part of life orientation. Jesus called this "entering the kingdom of God."

Warning: Do not confuse the metaphor "new level of consciousness" with New Age movement thinking or other contemporary distortions of biblical Christian thought. Like all metaphors, "level of consciousness" is not precisely synonymous with Jesus' term "kingdom of God." It is, however, one meaningful way to describe the psychological state of persons who enter the kingdom of God that Jesus described. Like all metaphors, "new level of consciousness" is a limited rather than a comprehensive description. The kingdom of God is far more than a personal state of mind; it is the entire realm of God's sovereignty—past, present, and future—both in the world that we can see with our eyes and in the world beyond that we cannot see. To say that the kingdom of God is *only* a psychological level of consciousness would imply that it has no objective reality outside our own thought patterns. According to the New Testament, the kingdom of God is an objective reality, not a subjective experience in our imagination that does not exist until we decide it exists.

Jesus' Twenty Megatruths

Whatever metaphor, description, or definition we prefer for Jesus' favorite theme—kingdom of God—examining all his statements reveals that he broke the bread of that phrase into twenty bite-sized pieces. Which of these twenty was the most important? All of them! Otherwise, would not he have used *eight* bite-sized pieces, or *seventeen*? We can think of these bite-sized pieces as Jesus' twenty *megatruths*.

As we read Jesus' words, our thinking unintentionally tends to reconstruct his teachings into an abbreviated, personalized version. Jesus' great mind could hold all twenty megatruths in view simultaneously. His followers can rarely manage more than two or three. Because of childhood training, personal experiences, the social conditions of our generation, and the spiritual perception lenses common in our particular culture, we tend to focus on a few of the twenty. Many of us, though we have read the New Testament, hardly know that the other sixteen or eighteen teachings of Jesus exist. If we do, we are sure that he barely mentioned them or that they are unimportant.

Our mentally abridged edition of what Jesus taught allows us to read the words and obtain only a piece of the Word—while the remainder stands in a stack of leather-bound pages on our mantel, waiting to be appropriated.

Get a picture of your own theological selectivity by completing, either individually or as part of a group, the questionnaire below.

PERSONAL OPINION QUESTIONNAIRE
REGARDING JESUS' TWENTY MEGATRUTHS

On the following list of Jesus' teachings, check the items that you feel are most important:

_____ 1. You experience new ways of thinking and behavior when you enter God's kingdom.

_____ 2. You enter God's kingdom only by a changed attitude of the heart, not by following a list of religious rules.

_____ 3. Concentrating your attention on Christ strengthens your ability to enter and experience God's kingdom in greater fullness.

_____ 4. Prayer strengthens your ability to enter God's kingdom and experience it more fully.

_____ 5. You are blocked from entering God's kingdom unless you turn away from self-centeredness.

_____ 6. Taking pride in your religious achievements makes it difficult to enter God's kingdom.

_____ 7. Financial wealth makes it more difficult for you to enter God's kingdom, because your money brings a false sense of power that distracts you from seeking something better.

_____ 8. Though self-concern is not your goal, you receive rich rewards by entering God's kingdom.

_____ 9. Entering God's kingdom gives you a sense of security that comes from believing your personal needs will be cared for.

_____ 10. Entering God's kingdom releases a new power in your life and thought processes that transcends the normal cause and effect patterns of your environment.

_____ 11. Entering God's kingdom enables you to live joyfully.

_____ 12. If you enter God's kingdom, you will continue to live in that consciousness beyond the time of physical death.

_____ 13. Entering God's kingdom gives you increased love and concern for other people.

_____ 14. Entering God's kingdom makes you less judgmental about other people.

_____ 15. Entering God's kingdom gives you a more forgiving spirit.

_____ 16. Entering God's kingdom gives you the desire to help other people enter it too.

_____ 17. If you want to enter God's kingdom, you must live a self-giving life.

_____ 18. If your thinking and actions become self-centered, you can disconnect from God's kingdom.

_____ 19. Failing to enter God's kingdom brings you negative results.

_____ 20. God's kingdom will at an unspecified future time become more fully and obviously manifested in the whole of creation.

Christians Are Similar, Yet Different

After completing the survey above, look at the "Annotated List of Jesus' Twenty Megatruths" found in appendix A. A group composed of pastors and church staff members who complete this survey and compare their selections will see more clearly the "why" behind their differences. We all start from exactly the same source material, but each of us selects a different emphasis. This explains the differences between theological conservatives and liberals. Jesus' teachings provide evidence for both viewpoints and everything in-between.

Denominational Differences: Ask five ministers and five adult Sunday school classes in five different denominations to complete the survey above. This will illustrate why all denominations say they base their beliefs on the Bible, yet come up with entirely different views and wonder why other Christians cannot see things as clearly as they do.

Internal Denominational Differences: National meetings of denominations are often a battleground between 10 percent of the delegates on the theological left and 15 percent on the theological right, with 75 percent watching from the bleachers. The various groups sincerely want to serve Jesus Christ but differ significantly on how to do that.

Generational Differences: Reading sermons or Christian education materials from earlier decades can feel like walking through a museum of Christian thought. These leaders, too, worked hard at presenting Jesus' ideas, but how different from ours they sound! Why? Theological selectivity! The experiences through which each generation passes on its way to maturity cause it to select those teachings that seem to need greater emphasis. This is why older and younger church members and ministers can disagree so radically, yet sincerely.

Cultural Differences: Different sociological groups inevitably concentrate on different points among Jesus' twenty teachings.

Which of Jesus' twenty teachings do you think the apostle Paul emphasized most? The answer is 3, 5, 12, 19, and 20.

Which of Jesus' twenty teachings do you think pastors and charismatic congregations emphasize most? The answer is 3, 9, 10, and 11.

Which of Jesus' twenty teachings do you think positive thinking and self-esteem pastors such as Robert Schuller emphasize most? The answer is 8, 9, 10, and 11.

Which of Jesus' twenty teachings do contemporary fundamentalists and evangelicals emphasize most? The answer is 8, 16, 19, and 20.

Which of Jesus' twenty teachings do you think most pastors in your denomination presently emphasize most? Are those items similar or dissimilar to your own personal list? (Your answer spotlights why you are comfortable or uncomfortable in your denomination.)

Mixing, Matching, and Mismatching

The theological fingerprints of pastors and staff strongly influence their sense of meaning and fulfillment in a particular congregation or ministry position. (When a ship captain sets the compass heading for east while the crew rigs the sails for west, the result is more stress than progress.) *Which of Jesus' twenty teachings do you emphasize in teaching, preaching, and ministry priorities?* Which of the twenty do leaders in your congregation or organization use as their guiding lights? Are the two lists similar or different? The degree of match or mismatch predicts joy or stress in your ministry experiences.

Whether a church leader is matched or mismatched with lay or staff leaders is difficult to see during job interviews or early months of working together. More often, a sense of congruence or incongruence evolves through time, conversations, and experiences. If possible, try to obtain objective measurements of theological similarities and differences at an early stage of the relationship. One pastor, for example, used the survey above, along with the annotated list in appendix A, in all the adult Sunday school classes during early months of her tenure. She then collated the answers within each class and shared the totals from each class with all of the classes during the weeks of a sermon series on Jesus' twenty teachings. This allowed older and younger generations to see their similarities and differences. The pastor benefited from seeing how her theological views compared with various age groups in the congregation. This increased sensitivity helped her to avoid several conflicts.

A business leader relates that decision making is easy when your values are clear. Values are also the basis for church leadership decisions. Nothing feels better than playing on a team where everyone is trying to move the ball toward the same goal. Few experiences are more stressful than working with a group whose values are moving them in opposite directions. A museum in Corpus Christi, Texas, contains an exhibit of a mockingbird skeleton. Inside the winged skeleton is a huge eggshell. The bird produced an egg too large to lay and died trying to lay it. A leader who emphasizes two or three of Jesus' teachings that do not match the theological selectivity of most people in his or her congregation or organization understands how that mockingbird must have felt.

The Fatal Flaw in Mission Statements

A ship that has no sense of direction is in trouble. A ship whose crew members want to go in several directions is in worse trouble. The trend toward developing a congregational vision statement and mission statement grew out of that foundation principle. The motto on one congregation's stationery is, "The Church With a Vision." Few congregations can accurately describe themselves that way. More often, a church has several visions. When the pastor's vision competes with several dozen unstated visions of the lay leaders, he or she is an unhappy camper and so are they.

The group process of drafting and agreeing on a vision statement and a mission statement forces values to the surface of consciousness and conversation. Unfortunately, congregations and church organizations that use business methods to develop vision and mission statements sometimes pay only faint lip service to theological issues. Not taking the time to agree on which of Jesus' twenty teachings we feel God is calling us to emphasize in this organization and this generation can produce a vision and mission statement that sounds great but nobody owns. Each newsletter and worship bulletin carries the agreed-upon statement; yet the lay and staff leaders go on trying to accomplish their private visions and missions, based on their personal theological choices from Jesus' twenty teachings. The clergy and staff leaders of such an organization will feel like the executives of a Detroit automobile plant whose various department heads are trying to manufacture airplanes, trucks, tanks, and cars.

Does your congregation have a one-sentence vision statement that describes what it would look like at the peak of its effectiveness? If not, lead your leaders in imagining that you are five years from now and your church or organization has reached the mountaintop of ministry success. If a *Wall Street Journal* reporter wrote an article describing your church at that ultimate moment, what would the headline say? That is your vision statement. What subjects would five or six paragraphs of that article cover? When your leaders agree on the topic sentences for those five or six paragraphs, you have your mission statement. (Most contemporary vision statements describe the optimum desired goal; mission statements outline what the organization does to achieve that goal.)

To begin this process, ask the governing board and key leaders to complete the megatruths questionnaire. Collate and print the total check marks for each of Jesus' twenty teachings (or list them on a chalkboard). Then give the leaders the annotated list from appendix A, which enables them to see how they are similar to and different from each other. Such a discussion may require two or three sessions, but that kind of Bible study shepherds a diverse group toward unity of spirit and purpose. A mission statement and vision statement based on a consciously selected focus from among Jesus' twenty teachings helps people to move from visions into vision. Such a process also helps to transform the coaches and players from a group into a team.

A prominent restaurant chain posts this vision statement in all its properties: "Our mission is complete guest satisfaction." Is that focus always attained? Probably not. But the staff team does not need lengthy debates about what target they are trying to hit.

An old adage says, "If you shoot at nothing, you will probably hit it." An addendum to that wisdom should say, If you shoot at everything, you will probably hit each other. Effective disciples of Jesus Christ try to follow their leader. Disciples that experience high satisfaction and low mental stress try to follow their leader while maintaining loving, caring relationships with each other. A crucial element in attaining that experience is finding or building a group that follows the same Jesus you follow.

CHAPTER 3

WHICH SPIRITUAL FOOD ENERGIZES YOU?

S teve is frustrated. He feels like a heart transplant patient who knows that his body is rejecting its source of life. Five years after seminary, the big dreams of those days have faded to a distant memory. Steve's ministry feels like a *Mission Impossible* episode with the happy ending deleted. He wonders what he can do to improve his feelings. Nothing, he thinks most days. A depressive sense of meaninglessness has settled over his mind like low-lying clouds stretching to every horizon. Trapped in a job so different from his expectations, he wonders if all pastors feel this way. Surely not, or they would not stick with it. "I guess it's just me," he thinks.

Differences That Make a Difference

Seminaries allow ministerial students just a few elective courses. All clergy need to know the basics of Bible, theology, Christian education, and church history. Their training is therefore more cookie-cutter than individualized. This should not surprise us. Physicians get a basic medical degree before they can specialize in psychiatry, pediatrics, general practice, or surgery. Lawyers get a basic law degree before they can specialize in tax law, estate planning, or corporate law.

For the same reason, academic training for ordained ministry cannot predict an individual clergyperson's satisfaction level in a particular congregation or ministry role (any more than sending lay staff members to Christian education workshops ensures that they will enjoy that role in a particular congregation). In all vocations, possessing the basic information and skills to do a job does not guarantee that you will want to do it. Clergy and church staff, like all other knowledge workers, begin moving in a general direction because of their personal sense of call to ministry. However, they obtain their *specific direction* from on-the-job experience.

Job satisfaction among clergy and lay staff arises from multiple sources, some of which are internal (within the psyche) and some of which are external (in the environment). On-the-job experience generates interaction between these internal and external causes. When the interaction is positive, a feeling of compatibility results. When the interaction is negative, friction results. Heat from that friction is called vocational dissatisfaction.

Clergy and lay staff members are highly aware of some of the internal predispositions they bring to their ministry roles. The *ministry model ideal* discussed in chapter 1 and the *theological viewpoint* discussed in chapter 2 are internal compasses of which their owners are highly conscious. However, some of their other internal predispositions are much more invisible. *Spiritual type*, for example, is a far less obvious determiner of job satisfaction. Many people get several years into their ministries before they become aware that some kinds of spiritual food energize them and other kinds feel like missing a meal.

Research by Urban Holmes III uncovered four types of authentic religious experience.[1] Most individuals readily identify themselves with one of Holmes' four types. When they hear them described, they usually recognize one of the four as the soil from which their most significant spiritual growth experiences have come. Everyone, at times, finds meaning in all four kinds of spiritual experience, but each individual feels truly at home in one of them. (This is a totally different paradigm from the well-known Myers-Briggs concept.)

Most congregations and organizations (usually without knowing it) provide one rather than four types of spiritual food. Church attenders strengthen this pattern by selecting (usually without realizing why) a congregation or organization that serves the kind of spiritual food they feel they need. Once located there, these attenders become leaders who further strengthen the focus of this one kind of religious environment and nurture. Congregations and religious organizations therefore tend to attract "our kind of people" and repel other types of people.

In the best-case scenario, a congregation's leaders feel genuinely tolerant about this natural selection process—making remarks such as "People should go to church where they feel spiritually comfortable." In the worst-case scenario, a congregation's leaders feel quite intolerant of this natural selection process—making comments such as "They just do not understand real Christianity." (This intolerance is expressed with approximately equal frequency by people in theologically fundamentalist congregations and people in theologically moderate and liberal congregations.)

The Four Religious Types

A car's steering wheel determines its direction. In people, the will (an internal volitional guidance system that heredity and environment influence but never totally control) determines life direction. Every kind of *meaningful* spiritual experience makes contact with the individual's will. Like a car's steering wheel, the will influences the person's choices to move his or her life in a new direction (or at least to believe that a new direction is resulting). Most people define a spiritual experience as devoid of meaning if it does not sufficiently touch their will so that it moves them in a new direction. Generally speaking, people tend to avoid repeated involvement in spiritual experiences that to them lack meaning (the ability to touch the will and change life direction).

Four different kinds of people define as *meaningful* four different types of spiritual experience. Summarizing each of these four with one word oversimplifies a complex phenomenon, but the four words listed below will help spotlight the distinctiveness of each type. Four different groups of people report that a spiritual experience is most likely to touch their will if it primarily involves one of the following:

1. Thinking
2. Feeling
3. Meditation
4. Action

When people say they did not find a church or a particular religious experience within a congregation meaningful, they mean that the type of spiritual food the church provided lacked the power to touch their wills and influence their life directions. Closer examination often reveals that the spiritual food served was for one or more of the other three kinds of people. It met someone else's needs but not theirs.[2]

Read the four descriptions below. *Which of the four kinds of spiritual food is your primary source of nourishment?* If the spiritual food you receive and serve each day in your ministry role does not match your spiritual type, the incompatibility will register itself in feelings of emptiness, frustration, or anger.

The Thinking Type: This kind of person reports that his or her will is best stimulated by spiritual thinking (these people think in order to feel). Such individuals find spiritual guidance in the words of Scripture, sermons, and position papers on ethical issues. "Thought content" is crucial for them. They are likely, for example, to examine the words of hymns to see if we are singing what we believe.

The Feeling Type: This kind of person reports that his or her will is best stimulated by spiritual feeling (these people feel in order to think). Such individuals find spiritual enrichment in music, heartfelt testimonials by persons whose lives God has touched, and engagement in personal evangelism efforts. "Emotional content" is crucial for these people. For example, they are likely to judge hymns by how the style and tempo make them feel rather than by word content and definition.

The Meditative Type: This kind of person reports that his or her will is best stimulated by spiritual meditation (these intuitive persons focus inward in order to think and feel). Such individuals find spiritual enrichment in contemplation and introspection. Sometimes called mystics, their prayer is largely an experience of hearing God speak to them rather than vice-versa. Many such persons publish inspirational and instructional material. They often find scant spiritual nurture in Western Protestantism, which may seem to them more like a social club than a God-focused group.

The Action Type: This kind of person reports that his or her will is best stimulated by involvement in spiritual actions (these people take action in order to think and feel). Such individuals find spiritual enrichment in service and idealistic crusading designed to transform society. For them, action is authentic theology and prayer. This definition causes many such individuals to find little spiritual nurture in organized religions—which they may accuse of "talking the talk but not walking the walk."

Each of these four spiritual types of people tends to find spiritual nurture in a different kind of congregation. Every denomination contains people of all four types, but most observers would agree with the following generalized summaries: Episcopal and Presbyterian congregations contain numerous thinking types. Southern Baptist and Nazarene congregations contain many feeling types. The Friends (Quakers) and Christian Science congregations contain many meditative types. Unitarian Universalists and United Church of Christ congregations contain many action types. To a great extent, this explains why churchgoers decide to switch denominations. It also explains why ordained clergy and lay staff decide to switch.

Side Dish Preferences

Each of the four types of people receives some secondary nourishment from one of the other three types of spiritual food. Read the following examples to identify your secondary source of spiritual nourishment.

- Some thinking types find spiritual benefit in an occasional meditative experience or involvement in an action-oriented crusade.
- Some feeling types receive spiritual benefit from action-oriented crusades. Other feeling types may find value in occasional meditative experiences.
- Some meditative types, if they possess an intellectual orientation, may enjoy writing and speaking the God-given visions they have obtained through quiet contemplation. Occasionally, the meditative type finds spiritual benefit in action-oriented crusades that live out the visions obtained in meditation (Joan of Arc is one example). Other meditative types obtain benefit from occasional spiritual feeling experiences such as music.
- Some action types use thinking experiences such as data collection to spiritual advantage—as a way to gather evidence for a betterment crusade or to increase self-esteem by having more knowledge. Many action types also benefit spiritually from an occasional feeling experience.

If your ministry position requires you to serve and receive your primary and your secondary source of spiritual nourishment, your job may feel extremely satisfying. What if your job provides your secondary source of nourishment but not the primary source? You may decide that you can tolerate your job because the less meaningful parts are interlaced with occasional flashes of meaning and value. Or, you may decide that secondary value spiritual food is not enough.

Generational Food Preferences

Sociologists have hotly debated "generational theory." Proponents say that history reveals four generational thinking and behavior types (each covering twenty to twenty-two years) that have recurred in dependable cycles since A.D. 1517, the dawn of the Protestant Reformation.[3] Other sociologists deny that the historical evidence is sufficient to support the existence of a four-generation cycle of recurring personality types.

Believers in generational theory see the four cycles of personality in the twentieth and twenty-first centuries roughly as follows:[4]

- **Crisis Era** (1925–1945), during which a communitarian spirit emerges to face social problems, and a secular crisis forges the iron of a single-minded unity in society. For Americans, this was the Depression and World War II.
- **Outer-Directed Era** (1945–1967), during which conformity and stability predominate, triumphant ideals are secularized, and great institutions are built. For Americans, this era climaxed during the Eisenhower years of economic growth and social stability.
- **Awakening Era** (1967–1989), during which cultural creativity increases, new ideals emerge, and cherished institutions and values are challenged or rejected. For Americans, this era was ushered in by the Vietnam War, racial unrest, and the economic inflation years of 1971–1981—during which a few Americans grew wealthy while middle-class income stayed flat in terms of real dollars.
- **Inner-Directed Era** (1989–2011), during which individualism, political fragmentation, and animosity predominate as secular problems increase and confidence in institutions fades. For Americans, this is a

period in which many individuals focus on spirituality as they despair of achieving the good life and stability in any other way.

Sociologists will continue to argue whether these twenty- to twenty-two-year generational themes appear in consistent cycles between 1517 and 1925. However, the most casual observer can see the differences among the four contemporary generations listed above. Two major causes produce these generational changes: (1) Teenagers and young adults identify the weaknesses and neglected issues that inevitably appear as their parents' generation carries good ideas to their extreme limits of usefulness. (2) Psychological, emotional, and intellectual stresses emerge when a changing culture generates new life experiences and forces a new generation to develop new ideas and ideals.

Long-term generational theory may or may not be accurate. (The truth may lie somewhere between the extremes of totally predictable cycles and random change.) However, churchgoing people among the four generations living today obviously correlate to a great extent with the four spiritual types nourished by four different spiritual foods:

- Crisis Era (1925–1945): Spiritual *action* type
- Outer-Directed Era (1945–1967): Spiritual *thinking* type
- Awakening Era (1967–1989): Spiritual *feeling* type
- Inner-Directed Era (1989–2011): Spiritual *meditation* type

As we observed above in our discussion of the secular differences between each generation, two factors cause changes in spiritual food preferences: (1) Weaknesses appear as the previous generation pushes good spiritual ideas to extreme limits. (2) New cultural expressions force each new generation to draw nourishment from a different spiritual food.

Regardless of whether we buy or reject the secular generation theory or the spiritual generation theory, church history reveals dominant kinds of spiritual food consumed during various periods over the past two thousand years:

- The *action* type of spirituality was most prominent during the Christian Crusades to free the Holy Land from Muslim control (1096–1270). The Christian social-action efforts that emerged in the 1960s are another example.

- The *meditative* type of spirituality saw its greatest popularity in the fourteenth century. The Friends' (Quakers') spiritual ancestors, the Friends of God, appeared then. Though always far less numerous than the other three types, meditative Christians exert strong influence through written material that speaks to contemporary issues important to all three of the other types.
- By far the largest percentage of contemporary American Christians fall into the two categories of *thinking* type and *feeling* type. From which of these two kinds of experience people obtain spiritual benefit depends to a great extent on the societal context in which they were immersed as youth and young adults.

Contrary to what many people believe, major changes in spiritual food preferences are caused less by new fads than by major changes in society (culture quakes). For example, many people find greater benefit in a "thinking type" of spirituality during periods marked by relative political stability, a dependable social order, and a strong sense of individual worth. Consider these examples:

- the third-century Egyptian period of Christian writing and thinking
- the twelfth-century Renaissance, during which society applauded learning and enlightenment
- the sixteenth-century flowering of humanism as a theological explanation of life
- the post–World War II period in America, when people placed great confidence in science and psychology to evolve a better and better "by our own bootstraps" life for everyone

Many people find greater benefit in a "feeling type" of spirituality during historical periods when the culture is unstable, the political order is crumbling, personal roles are poorly defined, and people feel a low sense of personal power to affect their future. Some of these times are:

- the fourth and fifth centuries, in which the Roman Empire's stabilizing influence collapsed
- the fourteenth century, during which the Black Death killed one-third of Europe's population

- the post–1965 period in America, a time of deteriorating confidence in scientific breakthroughs and rational thinking to solve personal and societal problems

Does not this help to explain the mainline membership decline and the evangelical membership growth? Once again, a large percentage of young adults find spiritual nurture in "feeling type" spiritual experiences. This is not happening because their denominations have changed but because their denominations have stayed the same while society was thrusting people into a different kind of life experience.

At the end of each generation, we see a "hinge of history," during which the extremes of religious nourishment and expression become obvious to the next generation and are gradually supplanted by a different type of spiritual food:

- If taken to extremes, the action type of spiritual experience becomes unrelenting tunnel vision—in which people (without knowing it) substitute frenetic doing for actual change in life direction. Their acting in order to think and feel replaces thinking and feeling. The next generation sees this flaw.
- If taken to extremes, the thinking type of spiritual experience becomes head trip rationalism—in which people (without knowing it) substitute thinking and discussing for actual change in life direction. Their thinking in order to feel replaces feeling. The next generation sees this flaw.
- If taken to extremes, the feeling type of spiritual experience becomes an exclusive pietism—in which people (without knowing it) substitute a desired emotional state for actual change in life direction. Their feeling in order to think replaces thinking. The next generation sees this flaw.
- If taken to extremes, the meditation type of spiritual experience becomes quietism—an extreme retreat from interaction with the world—in which people (without knowing it) substitute prayerful solitude for actual change in life direction. Their focusing inward in order to think and feel replaces thinking and feeling. The next generation sees this flaw.

The transitions between the four spiritual food preferences are not as distinctly observable as are the four secular generations' hinges. This blurriness is at least partially produced by the fact that every religious generation, no matter what spiritual food the majority of its members prefer, will also contain a sizable number of people with the three other spiritual food preferences.

Four Conclusions

Will these generational cycles keep repeating themselves in the future? Nobody knows. But we can derive at least four instructive conclusions from the available evidence:

1. Spiritual food preferences are determined far more by the spiritual extremes of the previous generation and by what is happening in society than by the instructions church leaders give people about the "right way" to experience God.

2. Most midsize and small churches serve primarily one kind of spiritual food and thus meet the needs of that type of person. A few extremely large churches provide all four kinds of spiritual food. Why have megachurches been emerging in America since 1965? The large organizational umbrella can far more easily provide diverse spiritual experiences. This also explains the effectiveness of many Roman Catholic parishes, whose large size provides such an umbrella.

3. As clergy and church program staff grow older, many of them can see why the spiritual food that best nourishes them (which they also recommend to others) is challenged as old-fashioned by a new generation of leaders.

4. When the type of spiritual food that energizes a clergy or lay staff member matches (a) the age range of the generation he or she is serving and (b) the congregation or ministry role in an organization with which he or she is engaged, job satisfaction is high. To the extent that one or both are mismatched, job satisfaction declines.

This is why the reformers and leaders of new religious movements are usually young people, generally in their twenties and early thirties. Only the younger leaders can perceive experientially what meets the needs of the generation currently coming into their adult years. Martin Luther was thirty-three when he nailed his Ninety-five Theses to a Wittenberg church's door and started the Protestant Reformation. Zwingli, the Swiss reformer, had by age thirty-six become one of the most noted preachers and leaders of the Reformed Church movement. John Wesley, founder of Methodism, was twenty-six when he organized his first Methodist Society.

Does the predominant spiritual food your congregation or organization serves and the spiritual food that your job requires you to serve energize you? Or does it make you feel like a ditch digger who had a glass of water for breakfast?

These differences matter, especially if you are also experiencing the major ministry model differences and the major theological differences described in chapters 1 and 2. These differences are even more frustrating because they are genuinely understood only by the clergy and lay staff who experience such gaps and are only vaguely recognized by colleagues whose spiritual food is congruent with what they receive and serve each day.

At the beginning of this chapter, we met Steve. Unlike many religious servants whose mismatched spiritual food source leaves them eternally hollow and empty, his story ends happily. He accepted a call to become the prayer minister for a huge congregation that averages five thousand in worship attendance. Now, he is serving and receiving in his daily work spiritual food that nourishes rather than depletes him.

CHAPTER 4

WHICH MINISTRY SKILLS HAVE YOU PERFECTED?

Ludwig van Beethoven, whom many consider the greatest composer of all time, was not a great conductor. During soft passages he often crouched on the floor. He sometimes jumped into the air and shouted to cue loudness at the beginning of a long passage, but nothing happened; he had miscounted and signaled too soon. As Beethoven gradually lost his hearing, the orchestra began ignoring his conducting and taking its cues from the first violinist. Finally, the musicians convinced him to give up conducting.[1]

Clergy and lay staff whose skills do not match their ministry positions rerun Beethoven's conducting experiences in two ways: (1) When the desire to accomplish a particular ministry is unaccompanied by the abilities needed in that position, their satisfaction levels plummet. (2) Many of the people with whom they serve begin wishing for another conductor.

Business consultants say that corporate employees who feel a strong sense of purpose and meaning experience the integration of four factors: passions, vision, environment, and talents.[2] That formula also applies to clergy and lay staff in congregations and organizations. *In which ministry skills are you most proficient?* A mismatch at this point can reduce to irrelevancy the perfect matches between the three other hidden determinants of leadership strength discussed in previous chapters: ministry model ideal, theological viewpoint, and preferred spiritual food.

51

Unfortunately, however, staff members often have difficulty recognizing a needed ministry skill's absence. The ego strength and personal optimism that usually accompany the sense of call to ordained or lay ministry roles can block accurate self-analysis. Then, too, lay leaders often assume that personal sincerity and the Holy Spirit will equip staff members for specific ministries regardless of their beginning skill levels. The evidence indicates that intelligence, desire to learn, and personal sincerity can often compensate for the lack of a particular skill, but not always. The abilities needed for different ministry roles are often as different as the skills required to be President of the United States and the skills needed to set interest rates at a level that avoids economic inflation or depression.

Forty Interconnected Skills

A little boy in a Scout uniform helped an aged nun across a slippery street after a New York ice storm. When they got to the other curb, he gave her a smart Boy Scout salute.

"Thank you very much," the nun said.

"Oh, you're welcome," the boy replied politely. "Any friend of Batman is a friend of mine."

Key leaders in every kind of business and nonprofit organization are sometimes victims of inaccurate stereotyping, some of which is negative but much of which is positive. People in church vocations get extra-large doses of what personnel managers call "the halo effect"—the inclination to assume that a job applicant can do everything well because she or he has a proven track record in one area. The spiritual nature of religious leadership quite naturally predisposes church members to ascribe Batman qualities to clergy and staff.

The multifaceted nature of clergy and staff roles increases the tendency toward overestimating their potential skill levels. Like shingles on a roof that overlap each other to get the job done, most church vocation positions use a variety of skills. Focus groups in Pittsburgh, Kansas City, and Los Angeles with pastors of small, midsize, and large churches from several denominations indicate that pastors and church staff need forty skills. They use each of these in varying degrees, depending on their ministry roles and circumstances. Broken into general categories, those forty skill areas are as follows:

Leadership Skills
- All aspects of leadership itself
- Coherent biblical and theological framework for pastoral leadership
- Ideas that help congregations shape a vision for the future

Diagnostic Skills
- Assessment of reality in the church and community
- Insight and skills specific to churches of different sizes

Personal Growth Skills
- Spiritual growth methods
- Ability to deal with personal psychological and spiritual problems such as family stress, failure, success, forgiveness, burnout, and depression
- Creativity
- Oral and written communications skills
- Time management

Interpersonal Relationship Skills
- Human relationship skills
- Listening skills
- One-to-one spiritual counseling as a pastor

Group Skills
- Aid in helping laity find and use their spiritual gifts
- Administration
- Organization and committee leadership skills
- Group process skills
- Conflict management
- Ability to deal with antagonistic personalities in the church
- Motivation skills
- Delegation skills
- Staff management

Ecclesiastical Skills
- Worship
- Preaching
- Music
- Prayer
- Evangelism
- Effective membership preparation methods and courses for adults and new Christians
- Bible study methods

- Sunday school methods
- Youth ministry
- Stewardship
- Budgeting, money management, handling memorial gifts and wills
- Community service
- Ideas for increasing the church's visibility as a helping and serving institution
- Ethics and justice issues
- Cross-cultural issues
- Methods for conducting weddings and funerals
- Contemporary office machinery technology
- World mission skills[3]

An old story tells about a lighthouse keeper along a bleak coast. His supervisor gave him sufficient oil for one month and told him to burn the light every night. One day a woman asked for some oil because she did not have enough to heat her home that week. He gave it. Then a farmer's son needed oil for a lamp so he could do his schoolwork. The lighthouse keeper gave it. Someone else needed oil for an engine. Before the end of the month, the lighthouse's oil tank ran dry and the warning signal went out. Three ships crashed on the rocks. More than one hundred people drowned. When the government supervisor investigated, the lighthouse keeper explained what he had done and why. "You had one task only," the official said, "to keep the light burning. Everything else was secondary. There is no defense."

The roles of clergy and staff are never that sharply defined. Their positions require doing several different things well. Can anyone have skill in forty ministry areas? Probably not. How do you select which twenty or fifteen lamps out of the forty to keep lit?

Clergy and staff find answers to that question in three primary ways: (1) research regarding the skills needed in various ministry roles, (2) feedback from people who observe their skills, and (3) self-assessment of ministry performance.

Research Insights

During those painful months in which pastor-congregation relationships deteriorate toward "involuntary termination," church members' complaints often fall into one or more of seven categories:

- "The pastor is a poor preacher," indicating inadequate public communication skills.
- "I just can't talk to the pastor," indicating inadequate listening skills.
- "The pastor has good ideas, but nothing seems to get done," indicating inadequate planning and follow-through skills.
- "The pastor doesn't visit people." This can take several forms, such as "He has been here five years and has never been in my house," or "She doesn't visit members who are in the hospital." Whatever the form, such complaints indicate inadequate communication of caring and concern for individuals.
- "The pastor looks seedy," indicating poor taste in clothing or inadequate personal hygiene.
- "The pastor can't get along with people," indicating poor human relationship skills.
- "The pastor doesn't always tell the truth," indicating high anxiety levels, manipulative tendencies, or a character defect.

Scientifically designed sociological research shows that the three skills that laypersons across the country view as the most essential for pastors are preaching, management/administration, and pastoral care. The three character values laypersons in churches of every size most admire in pastors are caring, cooperation, and honesty.[4]

Pastors who lack one or more of the three character values are less effective. However, possessing the three character values cannot compensate for the absence of one or more of the three skills: preaching, management/administration, and pastoral care. Sincerity is not enough!

Associate pastors and program staff also need the three pastor skills listed above but in a modified form that applies to their ministry specialty: communication skill (which may mean skill in teaching and personal communication rather than preaching), management/administrative skill, and caring skill. Like pastors, staff members in churches and religious organizations who lack the three character values of caring, cooperation, and honesty will face relationship stresses in their roles. Without those three character values, most of the people they serve will eventually cease to appreciate their high skill levels in communication, management/administration, and caring. On the other hand, having the three character values cannot compensate for the absence of one or more of the three basic skills. Sincerity is not enough!

In addition to those three skills and three character values, associate pastors and program staff need a seventh ingredient: relationship skill in working with their senior pastor or supervisor. The absence of this combination of skills and character values murders both the pastor's and the associate pastor's effectiveness and their feelings of job satisfaction. This relationship skill takes at least three forms:

1. Total allegiance to and affirmation of the senior pastor or supervisor. In congregations, this behavior includes unwillingness to listen sympathetically to parishioners' criticisms of the senior pastor, regardless of the senior pastor's imperfections. Effective staff members do not communicate personal agreement to complainers. Doing so automatically pulls staff members into a triangle-shaped conflict that reduces the value of their other abilities in the eyes of the senior pastor and the inner circle of church leaders. (Some people in the congregation will support and encourage staff members in such a conflict, but it eventually ends as a negative experience for all concerned.)

2. Positive self-identity and role-identity derived from a healthy self-image. This trait allows a staff member to laugh off putdowns that come to everyone who performs a vital specialized ministry but is not the senior pastor.

3. Humility that requires less public recognition than most senior pastors require. Content with less limelight than the senior pastor, they can feel comfortable playing the role John the Baptist played in relationship to Jesus (see John 3:30).

Several other personality factors that enhance clergy and program staff effectiveness are noted in chapter 8. However, none of the other personality qualities compensate for the absence of the seven noted above. Without those, effectiveness deteriorates and personal dissatisfaction escalates.

Feedback Insights

Someone said that feedback is the "breakfast of champions." Someone else added that feedback is the "mission impossible" for pastors. Neither statement is totally accurate. Feedback does not cultivate champions unless it is (1) drawn from truly representative samples of the people served, (2) accurately interpreted, and (3) appropriately utilized. Nor must feedback be the nightmare it often becomes during the annual performance review that is built into many clergy and staff contracts.

Such evaluation is greatly needed. Without it church vocation workers operate on insufficient information about their effectiveness. Without it, they tend to either overlearn or underlearn from the 6 percent of members in every congregation who are resident pastoral critics. Evaluation is biblical. Paul says, "Examine yourselves, to see whether you are holding to your faith" (2 Cor. 13:5). The book of Proverbs says, "An intelligent mind acquires knowledge, / and the ear of the wise seeks knowledge" (Prov. 18:15). Furthermore, evaluation goes on all the time. Failure to devise an appropriate system for hearing it does not prevent it from occurring.

Closing this feedback loop is full of dangers. The worst horror stories come from ill-advised efforts to get feedback at a time when things are not going well in the church. This inevitably leads to inaccurate data gathering. Regardless of how carefully a questionnaire is designed, if it is administered during a time of crisis, the responses will be a mixture of broken dreams about the church, head-chopping criticisms of the staff member, and honest analysis (given at the time when a clergyperson or staff member is least able to receive and use it constructively). After completing such a feedback process, expectations rise sharply among members of the congregation. They expect the pastor or staff member to instantly conform to their suggestions. When that does not happen, their anger may increase rather than decrease.

Bill Russell, a TV commentator for professional basketball, was covering a Boston Celtics game. They were winning the game by a wide margin, but Coach Bill Fitch was standing at the sidelines yelling at several players. Russell's partner in the broadcast booth asked why the coach was working his team over so strongly when they were doing so well. Russell replied that this was the perfect time to do it. They were "up" now and had confidence. They could take the criticism and improve their skills still more. That wisdom applies to evaluation in every field. Do it when things are going well. Do it in a scientifically effective manner. Take charge of it in ways that allow maximum potential for positive change. If done in those ways, feedback can become a breakfast of champions rather than mission impossible.

Peter Drucker, one of America's leading business consultants, says that leaders are neither born nor made. They are self-taught. That is especially true in churches. Although evaluation goes on all the time in every parish, pastors and staff need a system for evaluation that they can use on an annual or regular basis—one that is within their psychological comfort zone, one that feels acceptable to them. Otherwise, the flood of information goes right over the dam and down the river of lost opportunities. Clergy and staff seeking effective evaluation have two general alternatives to choose from. One is an opinion poll among members of the congregation's governing board. The other is a group process involving seven persons handpicked by the pastor for the feedback process. The seven-person feedback inventory is by far the safest and most effective. See appendix B for that procedure.[5]

Every staff member, no matter how sincere, has blind spots—behaviors that adversely affect ministry performance. Self-perception is important but never sufficient. The laypeople in your congregation or organization see these behaviors more clearly than you can. Those individuals are therefore your finest source of accurate assistance. They often feel but seldom express questions such as the following: How can they help you without hurting you? How can they be honest and kind simultaneously? How can they give you the truth without giving you pain? The seven-person system in appendix B allows your friends to avoid affirmation without honesty and judgment without kindness.

Self-Assessment Insights

Research by experts and feedback from others in the congregation or organization provides crucial insights, but some of our most valuable information comes from within. Self-assessment of skills by reflecting on personal experiences can distort reality. It may be rose-colored or overly negative. Yet self-assessment is the supreme court of how you feel about a ministry role and your likelihood of continuing in it.

Church vocation workers can self-assess in two primary ways: (1) by completing a "spiritual gifts inventory" and (2) by the positive and negative feelings resulting from their ministry role experiences.

Spiritual giftabilities. Completing one of the many types of spiritual gift inventories publicized during the last few decades reminds most people that they are to some extent like a computer.[6] Their cerebral software is preprogrammed for effectiveness in some jobs but not others. Without the appropriate mental and spiritual "giftability," no amount of experience or sincerity results in excellent job performance and satisfaction.

The Bible says that spiritual gifts are the special abilities God gives individual Christians. According to Ephesians 4:12, spiritual gifts are given "to equip the saints for the work of ministry, for building up the body of Christ." The basic New Testament texts regarding spiritual gifts are found in Romans 12:1-8; 1 Corinthians 12:1-27; 1 Corinthians 14:1-5; Ephesians 4:1-7, 11-16; and 1 Peter 4:8-11. These gifts are illustrated in numerous other texts throughout the Bible. Merely reading the list of definitions in appendix C, without completing a formal inventory, will give most people a general idea of their innate predispositions.

Spiritual gift inventories cannot tell you everything about your ministry skills, but they can spotlight basic inclinations. Such instruments can therefore (a) reduce the burnout that comes from forcing a square peg into a round hole and (b) increase the self-confidence and self-esteem that come from recognizing ministry roles in which you excel.

Personal experiences. According to an old story about Thomas Edison, his wife commented to him one evening, "You have worked too long without a rest. You need a vacation."

"Where will I go?" Edison asked.

"Decide where you'd rather be than anywhere else on earth and go there," she answered.

Edison thought a moment and said, "Very well, I will go tomorrow." The next morning he returned to his laboratory.

What you enjoy doing is not the full story. Some people like to do things at which they do not excel. Yet if you do not enjoy a particular job, are you likely to continue it for long and derive satisfaction from it?

Review the research insights and the skill categories in the feedback instrument in appendix B. Ask yourself what ministries you would want to do tomorrow if you had no financial needs and total discretion in selecting a ministry position. Your answer will not guarantee effectiveness and satisfaction in a particular ministry role. However, if you do not enjoy what you do, you are not likely to stick with it long enough or study it hard enough to become highly skilled at it.

Back to Which Basics?

In 1958, the Green Bay Packers won one game, lost ten, and tied one. During the previous ten years, the Packers had won thirty-four games and lost eighty-four. In 1959, the Green Bay team restructured and began concentrating on the basics of football: blocking and tackling. Over the next ten seasons, they won more than 75 percent of their games—a total of 148 victories—and became National Football League champions five of those years.[7]

People who excel at any endeavor concentrate on developing skill in its basics. Without focus, no amount of sincerity wins games. If Green Bay had concentrated on the basics of basketball, a turnaround could not have happened.

In what ministry skills do you excel? What ministry skills do you enjoy using? Those preferences and skills influence the kinds of games you win.

CHAPTER 5

WHICH LEADERSHIP TRAITS DO YOU POSSESS?

J ean had solid academic preparation for her specialized ministry role in a large congregation. Her IQ was high. Two years of experience had polished her technical proficiency. Six months after her start date her supervisor concluded that no amount of mentoring would remedy the deficiencies in her job performance.

Karen accepted another program staff position in the same congregation. She possessed neither formal education nor experience in this ministry role. Her IQ was adequate but not exceptional. After six months, church members were telling her supervisor, "She is the best we've ever had. I hope we can keep her forever."

These two biographies do not prove the irrelevancy of four highly respected predictors of vocational success: specialized skill, IQ, academic training, and experience. However, such stories illustrate that possessing those four qualities does not guarantee ministry effectiveness. A fifth quality, which some call leadership ability and others call "emotional intelligence,"[1] must accompany the first four. The fifth quality is so potent that it can, to some extent, compensate for the absence of the other four.

An explosive increase in leadership research during recent years signals the importance of that fifth quality. Business, government, and nonprofit sectors would like to define it. They could then test for its presence before hiring people and identify present employees whose aptitudes indicate that training will help them to have more of it. Bernard Bass and Ralph

Stogdill's *Handbook of Leadership* listed around three thousand studies in 1974, five thousand in 1979, and more than seven thousand studies by 1994.[2] Because leadership ability is so complex in structure, those seven thousand studies have not defined it in precise terms. The studies have, however, suggested that leadership ability is like a necklace with at least twelve diamonds. A pastor or church staff member can lack one of the twelve with few people noticing its absence. When six diamonds are missing, job stress increases. If eight are missing, vocational pain replaces job satisfaction. If all twelve are missing, the individual is usually a *former* church employee.

Study the twelve items discussed below. *Which of these classic leadership effectiveness traits are present in your daily attitude and behavior patterns?* In what ways would their absence reduce your effectiveness? In what ways would lacking one or more of them make irrelevant your academic training, IQ, specialized skills, and years of experience? In what ways would strengthening one or more of these twelve put more effectiveness into your present congregation or ministry role?

1. Excellence: High-quality ministry task performance and similar expectations of others. The people who most possess this leadership quality are always looking for it. They forever aspire to higher levels of achievement.

What causes this drive for excellence? Why do some people have this yearning and others lack it? Researchers are not certain. The drive for excellence is an inner flame kept burning by a combination of fuels, no one of which totally determines its brightness.

- Intelligence increases the likelihood of excellence but cannot guarantee it; many intelligent people do not reach for excellence.
- Perfectionism increases the likelihood of excellence but cannot guarantee it; many perfectionists who want to do it "their way" fail to see the limitations in their own performance standards.
- Experience increases the likelihood of excellence but cannot guarantee it; many experienced people are satisfied with mediocrity.
- Self-confidence increases the likelihood of excellence but cannot guarantee it; many self-confident people hop from subject to subject like gnats. They do not sufficiently focus their energies to excel in one or two specific ministries.

- High ethical standards increase the likelihood of excellence but cannot guarantee it; many highly ethical people accomplish little.
- Self-control increases the likelihood of excellence but cannot guarantee it; some self-controlled people are too rigid to consider new ideas.
- Self-motivation increases the likelihood of excellence but cannot guarantee it; many self-motivated people fire their lives like shotguns, aiming at everything in general but nothing in particular.
- Personality dominance increases the likelihood of excellence but cannot guarantee it; some dominant people are so abrasive that they drive their colleagues toward exits rather than excellence.

Research psychologists will continue to debate the relative strength of the several factors that make some people drive for excellence and other people satisfied with average or less. Whatever causes this difference in people, it powerfully determines whether their peers view them as leaders or nonleaders. An administrator who dictates dozens of letters each day showed her typist a flawed paragraph that needed changing. The typist responded, "I hoped you wouldn't catch that." The typist had many good qualities, including business school training, specialized skill, adequate IQ, and experience. The absence of a fifth quality—the drive for excellence—will keep her out of leadership roles.

2. Objectivity: The ability to accurately assess reality. Leaders never make perfect scores on this test, but they consistently get higher grades than the people they lead. Some business writers say that defining reality is job one of every CEO. Wherever it ranks in the list of essential leadership qualities, clergy and staff who frequently fail to accurately define reality walk up stairs of sand in their journey toward effectiveness.

High IQ contributes to but does not guarantee high objectivity. Possessing high levels of specialized knowledge does not equate with objectivity. In the field of science, for example, intelligent Ph.D.'s sometimes get so locked into historic ways of thinking about a scientific issue that their objectivity blurs—which explains why so many scientific breakthroughs come from the fringes of a scientific community rather than its core.

Carl Jung asserted that everyone has an innately preferred position on each of four personality scales: Extroversion-Introversion, Sensing-Intuitive, Thinking-Feeling, and Perceiving-Judging.[3] A person's location on the Thinking-Feeling scale influences his or her "objectivity quotient."

Extreme "Feeling" people tend to base decisions on how the people close to them feel. Extreme "Thinking" people tend to base decisions on factors such as efficiency, present goals, and the positive cost-benefit ratio. Effective leaders are sensitive to other people's feelings, but they seldom score at the extreme "Feeling" end of the scale.

People in ministry positions must exert leadership among leaders. That requires an objective assessment of reality. The habit of holding up a wet finger to the wind of close friends' opinions is not enough.

3. Innovation: The ability to create, either alone or with the help of others, effective new ways to accomplish the organization's ministry, solutions to problems, and means of dealing with changing circumstances. Innovators never stop learning and growing. They break through their natural fear of change and take risks to make things better, exercising initiative in ways above and beyond their stated job responsibilities.

Biographies of innovative leaders sometimes make their lives seem like forty-year parade routes accompanied by public oohs and aahs. A closer look disintegrates that myth. Most innovators move *against* the tide of the majority's opinion, which usually resists rather than affirms change, at least in its first stages. Innovators must therefore possess sufficient self-confidence to move ahead despite negative comments.

4. Persistence: The tenacity to keep driving toward goals. People who risk making changes not only succeed more often; they also fail more often.[4]

Effective leaders are so completely committed to their personal visions and projects that they see setbacks as stepping stones rather than dead ends. When they fail, they forgive themselves and move on. When they fall down, they pick themselves up, figure out why, and give the game another shot (with the added advantage of having learned from a mistake). An inner Teflon coating gives them higher than average tolerance levels for frustration. They keep rowing toward their goal against waves of ambiguity and new problems.

5. Communication: The ability to express ideas and goals clearly, in ways that minimize misunderstanding. John Gardner defines leadership as "the process of persuasion and example by which an individual (or leadership team) induces a group to take action that is in accord with the leader's purposes or the shared purposes of all."[5] Communication skill is the foundation of leadership persuasion. Although few leaders excel at all forms of communication—conversation, speeches, and writing, for example—every leader should be capable of expressing ideas and goals clearly.

Ineffective communication takes three primary forms:

- *Overcommunication that lacks focus.* The world's first newspaper appeared in 59 B.C. Julius Caesar, the first publisher of *Action Journal,* posted it throughout the city of Rome. Similar to present-day tabloids, it printed social and political news, births, marriages, deaths, and the highlights of Colosseum sporting events. Some poor communicators sound like an entire newspaper instead of an article focused on a subject. They say a great deal about everything, but when they finish many people ask, "What was the point?" In leadership communication, less is often more.
- *Unclear communication that creates confusion.* The story about a florist whose business failed indicates that a pattern of mixed messages was the primary cause. On one occasion, for example, he sent the flowers for a wedding to a local funeral and vice-versa. The note with the flowers to the people getting married read, "Our deepest sympathy to both of you." The card with the funeral flowers read, "Good luck in your new location." Effective communicators do more than focus on one subject; they are clear and accurate about it.
- *Insufficient information that precipitates paranoia or misunderstanding.* When members of congregations or organizations are consistently uninformed about major issues, their imaginations invent and distribute information to fill the vacuum. Some of that information is accurate. Much of it, manufactured out of their best hopes and worst fears, is highly distorted. Persuasive leaders know that the time they spend informing people of important issues actually saves time. Such communication reduces the grapevine distribution of inaccuracies that will require three to five times as much of the leader's energy to correct later on.

Someone wrote a pastor a note praising his ability to communicate complex religious issues with clarity. "Thank you for always putting the cookies on the bottom shelf," the parishioner said. Communication is a crucial skill for every kind of leader. Many achievements live or die by the leader's skill in mouth-to-ear resuscitation.

6. Inspiration: The ability to express vision, high ideals, goals, and hope in ways that move others toward new thinking and actions. Great dreams can generate incredible energy but only when shared in inspiring ways. Effective leaders go beyond clarity; their vision package is wrapped in enthusiasm, conviction, and sincerity. They consistently convey an optimism that labels themselves and others as winners, despite all odds.

Inspiration is an especially crucial quality in times of organizational stress. An old saying about golf reminds us that the real test is not in keeping out of the rough but in getting out once you are in. Leaders can inspire people who are in the rough to move beyond it. They see and communicate to others extraordinary opportunities in ordinary circumstances.

In the early, difficult days of Federal Express, Fred Smith, the founder of the company, faced a wall of obstacles. Thirty million dollars in debt, he was indicted for defrauding a bank, he was sued by his own family, and he nearly lost his job as chairman of Federal Express. Yet he inspired such loyalty among his employees that some of the van drivers pawned their watches to buy gasoline so they could get their packages to the airport on time.[7] Effective leaders in every kind of organization have inspirational qualities that motivate common people to do uncommon things.

7. Caring: A genuine interest in people, evidenced not just in an extroverted personality but in concern for their needs. Peter F. Drucker, guru of the business management world, reminded clergy and students in an address at Claremont School of Theology in California that the central purpose of a cleric is the congregation and the central purpose of a congregation is the person. Compassion for persons is therefore a religious leader's unique keynote.[8]

Caring alone, devoid of the other eleven leadership qualities, cannot make people effective. But religious leaders who lack the caring quality will eventually be disliked by so many people that their leadership light will dim to firefly intensity. Many business leaders are respected but not liked. In religious organizations, however, few leaders survive on respect alone. Their followers must also like them, and that begins when the leaders like their followers.

One of the prime ways church leaders communicate caring is by being fully present in conversations with people, while enmeshed in several fast-lane job responsibilities. Effective religious leaders can do two things at once—care about organizational goals and care about people. Contemporary social scientists call these two functions "structure behavior" and "consideration behavior." Whatever we call this juggling act, people who cannot do both cannot excel as church leaders.

8. Sensitivity: The ability to understand people and their reaction patterns. Caring about people is not enough; effective leaders also have the capacity to see things from another's perspective.

Someone estimated that 50 percent of all first-term missionary failures are attributable to some failure in human relationships.[9] One pastor wrote in his prayer journal, "Sensitivity to feelings is as important as IQ and ideas. Stop trying to succeed and start trying to relate." In every ministry role, the apostle Paul's advice still applies: "We exhort you, brethren, admonish the idlers, encourage the fainthearted, help the weak, be patient with them all" (1 Thess. 5:14).

Sensitivity must include the recognition of manipulative behavior in others. A pastor described how he made a mistake in accepting a congregational call: During the interview process, the pastor had been moved by a pulpit committee member's extremely emotional speech expressing his burden for their church's need of a pastor with this candidate's ability. The committee member was apparently so overcome with emotion that he broke down and cried and had to leave the room. Later, the pastor learned that the man was head of the local college's drama department. Sensitivity means much more than a leader's willingness to accept every word and behavior at face value. Sensitive leaders achieve a high level of assessment accuracy in their people watching and relationships.

9. Receptive listening: The willingness to gather information from others before making judgments. Effective leaders convey a "why not?" attitude by listening carefully to people who bring them a new idea or proposal. They operate on the assumption that this person has a good idea—unless further conversation demonstrates otherwise. People who lack this receptive listening trait convey the feeling early in the conversation that the individual's new idea could not possibly be a good one. Thus, they block its expression, often by citing reasons why it would not work or giving a similar illustration from the past that did not work.

Nonreceptive listening has three negative consequences:

- People feel personally rejected instead of feeling that the leader likes them and appreciates their suggestions.

67

- People stop communicating any ideas to the leader, thus cutting him or her off from a major source of grist for the innovation mill.
- The leader becomes disconnected from what people in the congregation or organization are thinking about its ministries.

In their conversations, effective leaders do two things: they ask questions, and they listen. This makes people like them, respect them, and want to bring them information. The more the leader listens, the more people feel affirmed. The more questions the leader asks, the more people perceive him or her as genuinely interested. The one basic need that everyone brings to every conversation is the need for *acceptance.* That psychological term is nearly identical in meaning to the biblical word *grace* (forgiveness of imperfections). Leaders who communicate acceptance by listening and asking questions thereby accumulate the power to achieve many things. Leaders who lack that skill reduce their authority and eventually fail at many things.

Along with the two positive conversational behaviors of listening and asking questions, effective leaders tend to avoid three negative patterns: (1) gossip, (2) giving unrequested advice, and (3) sarcasm. An old Scottish saying sums up how people react to those three conversational patterns: "His absence is good company." Unfortunately, most people who heavily pepper their conversations with one or more of those three negative elements often see them as virtues rather than liabilities. "I call a spade a spade," one man says. "I hate to sound critical, but it's the truth," another says after every sarcastic remark. Such individuals are often colorful and sometimes interesting, but they are seldom leaders.

10. Forthrightness: The courage to sensitively communicate concerns to others, even when there is risk of alienation. Insensitive people often fail to distinguish between forthrightness and abrasiveness. Forthright people exercise their skill only on rare occasions. Abrasive people use their pattern constantly. Generally speaking, forthright people have earned the right to express a straightforward concern because they have a long-term, positive, foundational relationship with an individual or group. Psychologists would call this a trust relationship. This usually requires several interactions involving objectivity, caring, sensitivity, and receptive listening. By definition, a friend is someone who can be honest with you without breaking the relationship. Forthright leaders have that skill.

Mel Brooks once told a story about a man who suffered from a compulsion to tear paper. After several years of psychoanalysis, John was no better. His family was losing hope. So John's parents took him to a new therapist. Instead of listening to him for hours, the therapist walked John around the room, talking quietly to him. In one session, John was cured. One year later, he was still okay. Overcome with curiosity, John's mother phoned the therapist and asked what he said to John in that one turning-point session. The therapist said, "I told him, 'Don't tear paper.' "

Most leadership change is facilitated by receptive listening and asking questions. However, some kinds of change happens only through forthright talking. Effective leaders know when to do which. They build the prerequisite relationships necessary to forthrightness. They know how to be direct in ways that reduce the risk of alienation.

11. Effective conflict management: The ability to help people work through emotionally charged differences of opinion in ways that build consensus and team spirit. The name of a Greenwood, South Carolina, congregation sounds like an oxymoron: Tranquil United Methodist Church. Unless its founders named it after a street, village, township, county, lake, or wooded area, they were dreaming the impossible dream. Is any organization or church with more than one member continuously tranquil?

In describing Jackie Robinson, the first black major league baseball player to break the color barrier by playing for the Brooklyn Dodgers, a newscaster said that he had the stamina of spirit to deflect the arrows of criticism that came with the role. All effective leaders have some of that stamina. Leaders take people in directions they would not otherwise go. Some people will not want to make the trip. They prefer the security of mediocre but familiar territory. To be a leader is therefore to experience some conflict.

Effective conflict management, however, goes several miles beyond the ability to tolerate personal criticism. Conflict managers can continuously assess circumstances, work within the limits of their organizational structure, and stay in communication with people of diverse opinions. In a continuously evolving landscape they function in ways that meet and defeat the dragons of controversy, which could deter the organization from achieving its ministry goals. Leaders never feel that they do this perfectly, but they always do it adequately. (When they stop doing it adequately, they are no longer leaders.)

12. Effective time management: The ability to select priorities that fit a church or organization's ministry goals and consistently

focus attention and energy on those goals. Time management is actually goal management and self management, with a few efficiency habits thrown in.

Here is a short course on time management in five imperatives:

1. Clarify your objectives.
2. Establish priorities that match your objectives.
3. Break the big jobs into little pieces and start on one of the little pieces immediately.
4. Clean up your paperwork daily.
5. Learn to say no to important requests that do not fit with your objectives.[10]

In ministry roles, however, time management is not that simple. Ministry roles usually contain far more discretionary time than secular jobs. Most people in ministry roles also have more latitude to set goals and lead in directions of their own choosing. Therefore, chapter 10 will translate those five short course imperatives into a thirty-six-point course on ministry time management, moving beyond secular principles to address the distinctive characteristics of clergy and program staff roles.

Can Leadership Be Taught?

How can people acquire these twelve leadership traits? Can they be taught in a leadership course? The debate about that question's answer will continue. Much evidence indicates the accuracy of four different answers: yes, no, maybe, and sometimes.

Yes! If medical schools can teach brain surgery, leadership skills are surely teachable. An old anecdote says a stranger in a small village asked an old-timer, "Were any great men born here?"

"No," the villager replied, "only babies."

All great leaders are born without a knowledge of leadership principles. They start as babies. They must learn how to lead. What can be learned can surely be taught.

No! Leadership traits cannot be taught to people who lack the basic psychological predispositions and reflexes that effective leaders possess. (Carpenters cannot build houses on nonexistent foundations.) Nor can leadership traits be taught to unmotivated people. Adopting positive leadership habits happens only with the willingness to drop negative leadership habits. Such dramatic changes come only to highly motivated people. In that sense, leadership cannot be taught by others; it is self-taught.

Maybe! Leadership instruction is a messy science. If early ministry experiences providentially put highly motivated, genetically equipped people into circumstances where they have access to a competent, willing mentor, the right kind of crisis can mold those components into effective leadership traits. In this respect, the ability to teach effective leadership traits is outside the control of the most capable and highly motivated teacher. Whether leadership can be taught depends on the convergence of a constellation of factors over which no teacher can gain control.

Sometimes! Leadership traits sometimes appear in people who lack formal educational background. (Abraham Lincoln is a prominent example.) More often, however, leadership blossoms in people who have adequate preparation, a motivating environment, encouraging models to watch, caring mentors to advise them, an unending passion to learn, and opportunities in which to practice. Sometimes these factors are all present; sometimes one or more of them is missing. That unpredictable, uncontrollable combination greatly determines whether people develop or fail to develop leadership skills.

On the present page of church history, these crucial components seem more often to coalesce around staff members in the large teaching churches than in the typical career evolvement pattern of seminary education, small parish, larger parish, and so on. This explains why so much effective ministry is accomplished by part-time laypersons whose only formal training is an occasional workshop or seminar. Although their training does not occur in the formal, classic setting, such staff persons are exposed to the basic ingredients from which they can learn and develop leadership traits.

Do you possess a high level of all twelve leadership traits listed above? If so, you are already in a leadership position or are on the fast track toward one; that is, of course, if you possess the other nine essential leadership strength components that suit you for the particular congregation or ministry role in which you are presently serving. Leadership traits cannot guarantee ministry effectiveness—any more than ministry skills devoid of leadership traits can make you effective. Ministry is a complex art containing many separate dynamics. Leadership traits are only one part of that art.

CHAPTER 6

WHAT SIZE IS YOUR BEHAVIOR?

During a rare twenty-inch snowstorm in San Antonio, Texas, one waitress remarked about a customer, "He thinks he knows everything about driving on ice because he grew up in Wisconsin."

Past experiences both help and hinder people. They help because they provide invaluable skills and insights. They hinder because they mold behaviors into a fixed pattern that may or may not be effective under a different set of circumstances. The San Antonio driver from Wisconsin knows how to drive on ice. But he does not know how to drive on ice in a city where the other drivers do not know how to drive on ice.

Reflexive behaviors based on past experience are especially inadequate when church leaders relocate to congregations or organizations of a different size. Some of the leaders' past experiences are assets; others are liabilities. During their first eighteen months in a new location, leaders often experience considerable stress while trying to figure out which ingrained behavior patterns to keep and which to discard.

Effective leaders in different sized congregations exhibit behavior patterns consistent with and formed by their group's size. It is possible to classify congregations, based on their average morning worship attendance, approximately as follows:

1–35 attenders
36–70 attenders

> 71–120 attenders
> 121–170 attenders
> 171–300 attenders
> 301–450 attenders
> 451–700 attenders
> 701–900 attenders
> 901–1,800 attenders
> 1,801–3,000 attenders
> 3,001–10,000 attenders
> 10,001 or more attenders

At the practical level, however, most church leaders do not need to slice their knowledge so thin. They can understand and deal with most of the stresses induced by moving from one size congregation to another by grouping the twelve classifications noted above into three general categories:

> 1–100 morning worship attenders (small)
> 101–300 morning worship attenders (midsized)
> 301 or more morning worship attenders (large)

To a great extent, the behavior patterns in small, midsized, and large churches apply to all types of religious organizations, not just congregations. The numbers are not identical. For example, a small church choir usually consists of twelve to fifteen people. A midsized church choir has fifteen to forty people. A large church choir has more than forty people. Yet people in other kinds of religious organizations will see great similarity between the behaviors of participants in their groups and the church behavior patterns outlined in this chapter.

Clergy and lay staff significantly increase their leadership effectiveness when they (a) understand the differences in behavior patterns among the three congregational sizes and (b) integrate the appropriate leadership behaviors into their emotional reflexes. Having the right ministry skills is not enough. Possessing the twelve classic leadership traits noted in chapter 5 is not enough. Effective clergy and program staff also must behave in ways that fit the size of their congregation or religious organization.

Lifestyle Characteristics

Sociological observations in small, midsized, and large congregations reveal at least seven different lifestyle characteristics. Review the seven lifestyle characteristics outlined in this chapter. *Which of the three behavior patterns do you characteristically use—small, midsized, or large?* Do your behavior patterns fit the lifestyle characteristics of your congregation or organization? Your answers to those questions reveal another major component of your leadership effectiveness and personal satisfaction level.

1. Different Priorities

The priorities in small churches (those with less than one hundred in average worship attendance) focus on *relationships.* Small churches resemble extended families, whose members emphasize doing everything as one group. In small churches, people matter more than performance. Thus, when a ten-year-old boy plays the viola in the worship service, the attenders overlook his musical imperfections. Like the boy's grandfather sitting on the back row, left side, everyone appreciates the youngster's sincere efforts. They know him personally, so the boy is more important than the quality of his performance.

The priorities in large churches (those with three hundred or more in average worship attendance) tend to focus more on *quality of performance* than on relationships. Few large-church attenders would personally know a little boy who plays the viola in worship. Therefore, unless the boy was an outstanding musician, many of them would view his special music contribution as "inappropriate for this setting." Many large-church attenders are seeking quality programming for themselves and their children. Thus, they have low tolerance for any worship service component that lacks professionalism. These expectations concerning high quality extend to every aspect of congregational life.

Which of these priorities do people in midsized churches (those with one hundred to three hundred in average worship attendance) emphasize? *Both,* which is why midsized churches are often called the awkward size. Many midsized-church attenders come from previous experiences in small churches. They are looking for *quality relationships,* a pastor who stops by for home visits, and the intimacy of belonging to a small group. Many other midsized-church attenders come from previous experiences in large churches. They are looking for *quality programs,* well-organized activities, and highly professional leadership. This explains why the midsized-church pastor needs superb conflict management skills. Midsized-church pastors are, of necessity, excellent conflict managers.

This combination of priorities—quality relationships and quality performance—also explains why meaningful programs are so important to midsized-church attenders. The effective midsized church is a group of small groups. The attenders with small-church backgrounds appreciate the intimacy of small-group experiences provided by the women's organization, men's organization, adult Sunday school classes, youth groups, sports leagues, and so on. The attenders with large-church backgrounds appreciate the performance quality of one or more sections of their midsized congregation.

The priorities in each of the three church sizes can be summarized as follows:

- Small Church: People Relationships
- Midsized Church: Meaningful Programs
- Large Church: Quality Performance

The leadership behaviors that fit the priorities in the three congregational sizes can be summarized as follows:

- Small Church: Chaplain
- Midsized Church: Y Director (YMCA, YWCA)
- Large Church: Corporation President

The value church attenders place on these leadership behaviors can be seen clearly in typical early conflicts in the three church sizes. An early warning sign of discontent among small-church members comes in the form of statements such as, "I'm not sure she cares about people." (If we are in the people business and our pastor is not good at that, we have a big problem.) An early warning sign among midsized-church members comes in the form of statements such as, "When Pastor Smith was here, we had thirty kids in the high school youth group; I understand only four kids are attending now." (If our pastor cannot produce meaningful programs that people want to participate in, we have a big problem.) An early warning sign among large-church members comes in the form of statements such as, "We used to run five hundred in morning worship; I don't think we have two hundred these days." (If our pastor cannot deliver the quality that collects a decent crowd at our major gatherings, we have a big problem.)

These three different priorities of three different congregational sizes—and the different leadership behaviors required to honor these priorities—explain why national research across denominational lines indicates that pastors in three sizes of churches prefer three kinds of continuing education. Pastors of small churches prefer to discuss (a) technical details of how to do various ministry tasks with limited finances and (b) various types of pastoral concern for individuals in the congregation. Pastors of midsized churches prefer to discuss (a) various types of church programs and (b) stresses related to conflict management among church groups and individuals. Pastors of large churches prefer to discuss (a) the importance of setting the vision for the congregation and (b) the importance of skill in managing staff. These differing interests, driven by the differing behaviors essential to achieving different priorities, explain why so many pastors complain about the meaninglessness of denominational clergy meetings. Geographical commonalities cannot bridge the three different mission fields and three different languages clergy must speak in order to be effective.

These three kinds of priority-driven behaviors also explain why pastors often experience eighteen to twenty-four months of stress when they relocate across invisible boundary lines of church size. Skills perfected in a smaller or larger church are inadequate in the new circumstances of a different sized group. The pastor must develop new behaviors while discarding some previously effective emotional reflexes.

An old story describes a traveling theater group that often performed a different play each night and sometimes two different plays each day. One afternoon, the exhausted lead actor forgot his lines. When he got no help from the prompter standing in the wings, the actor froze. "What's my line?" he whispered desperately.

"What's the play?" asked the prompter in equally desperate tones.

Clergy and program staff leaders experience similar frustration when their behavior fits the priorities of the church size they once served, the size of church they wish they served, or the size they unconsciously try to make their church fit.

2. *Different Pastoring*

Small-church parishioners expect a close personal relationship with their pastor and his or her family. The pastor of one such congregation was hearing good advice from God when he wrote in his daily prayer journal, "Care about your parishioners as persons (their problems and perspectives). Avoid the temptation to view people as tools to help accomplish your pet projects. Do not make home visits with the purpose of asking people to assume a church responsibility. Make individual caring your goal, and the people will help you achieve your church goals."

The majority of large-church parishioners expect to know their pastor primarily through large gatherings such as worship, funerals, weddings, fellowship dinners, crisis moments in the hospital, and newsletter articles. Effective large-church pastors therefore concentrate on delivering a caring presence at these brief but crucial times. They also know the value of a well-written column in each issue of the church newsletter. (Research indicates that most people read the pastor's column in the church newsletter, even if they read nothing else.) For many large-church attenders, the pastor's newsletter article is the way they can know their pastor's goals and personal opinions on issues.

What do parishioners in midsized churches want from their pastor and staff? Both quality relationships and quality performance, which presents a tough challenge for leaders of midsized congregations. People want close personal relationships, plus the excellent preaching and leadership ability essential to achieving great ministry goals. At about the 150 average worship attendance mark, the pastor must move beyond the skills needed to personally care about individuals and develop the skills to care about people in groups and help people in groups care about one another. Individual pastoral caring still happens, but it must take a variety of new forms:

- Some midsized-church pastors develop care teams of twelve to eighteen persons. Such a team meets monthly with the pastor and supplements the pastor's caring contacts at times of hospitalization, bereavement, and personal crisis.[1]
- Many midsized churches establish a "Care Line" by securing an additional telephone line attached to an answering machine. Each morning the senior pastor records two minutes of congregational information, such as funeral service announcements, names of people in the hospi-

tal, times of meetings and events that day, a scripture reading, and a prayer. This procedure enables a pastor to communicate caring to a large group in a short time.

- Most midsized-church pastors find that accessibility becomes as important an issue as home visits. Many such pastors therefore develop a pattern of being in the office for a specific block of hours each day (perhaps from 9 o'clock in the morning until noon). The pastor communicates to church members his or her accessibility by phone or personal visits during the specified time block on most days (in addition to accessibility by phone at other times).
- As part of daily devotions, many pastors move through the church membership list, praying for individuals in five different families each day. (Some pastors write a note to the families for whom they will pray that particular week.)

Colin Powell describes his admiration for a particular leader this way: "Tough and energetic in pursuing his goals, yet thoughtful and kind in his dealings with people."[2] All pastors need that mix, but the differing ways those traits are delivered depends more on the church's size than on its history or on its present circumstances.

3. Different Personnel

Small churches rely heavily on lay volunteers for getting things done. At the other end of the size spectrum, large churches rely far more on paid professional staff, who lead lay members in accomplishing ministries. In the middle of the size spectrum, midsized churches use a mixture of paid and volunteer staff, working through lay committees that may or may not depend on the leadership of paid staff members. This makes leading midsized churches especially complex. Some of the members expect to operate autocratically and independently of staff leadership (often due to their small-church background). Other members expect the staff to tell them all the details of what to do and how to do it (often because of their large-church experiences).

The core activities of every church involve achieving ministry objectives, maintaining a positive internal congregational climate, and making the adjustments necessary to adapt to a changing community environment. Small churches accomplish these core activities primarily through the individual relationships between pastor and members. Midsized churches accomplish these core activities primarily through the relation-ships between pastor, program staff, and the committees. Large churches accomplish those core activities primarily through the relationships be-tween the senior pastor and the program staff (who, in turn, lead lay leaders in ministry accomplishments).

Casey Stengel, the great baseball coach-philosopher, reportedly said that it's easy to get good players, but getting them to play together—that's the hard part. Pastors in every church must possess personnel manage-ment skills, but they exercise their skills in different ways in different sized churches.

4. Different Programming

Small-church attenders expect minimal programming, often consisting of worship, Sunday school, choir, youth activities, and a women's organi-zation. Large-church attenders, by contrast, expect a cafeteria of program-ming that meets the spiritual, emotional, social, and physical needs of persons at every age and stage of development. Midsized-church atten-ders expect either a short or a long programming menu, consistent with their prior church size experiences. Some are satisfied with a strip-mall church offering five or six programs. Others expect the dozens of options available in a shopping-mall church.

5. Different Participation

Small-church attenders expect everyone to participate in every gather-ing; any absence is a matter of concern. This unwritten contract is so strong that small-church attenders assume that missing persons are out of town, ill, angry, or dead. In their next conversations with absentees, members will attempt to discern which, so that the other members can take appropriate caring actions.

Large-church leaders, by contrast, expect elective participation habits. Members who do not attend everything are not viewed as disloyal or alienated. The large church is like a university that offers many courses, not like the second grade where everyone must master identical subjects.

Midsized-church attenders tend to want both kinds of participation. Some of them feel a bit guilty if they do not participate in every activity. Other midsized-church attenders expect to pick and choose among church activities, involving themselves in some and disregarding others.

6. Different Procedures

Someone quipped that wherever two or three are gathered together in God's name, there is politics. That cynical remark overstates a potential danger. Politics (another way of saying "procedures for authority, control, and decision making") exist anywhere two or more people gather for any reason whatever. Church politics is the art of working together to build and maintain positive ministries. Church leaders should not, therefore, strive to eliminate politics; rather, they should develop a political system that fits their congregation's size.

The English language has 40 different sounds. However, the ways to combine those 40 sounds total 550.[3] The procedural differences required for different sized churches are not that numerous, but leaders who apply the wrong one can create great pain (both for themselves and for their congregations). For example, small-church attenders expect their high involvement levels to give them strong ownership and control of decision-making procedures. Thus, the governing body meetings in small churches often have the emotional feel of a town-hall gathering in a small New England village. Everyone has equal input, and people not present at the meeting often exert strong influence. The question, "What will Joanne think of this decision?" recognizes that a majority vote by the board does not always equal a fait accompli. One layperson can veto a unanimous decision, if he or she is a key influence (authority figure). Most small churches give more congregational decision-making authority to key laypersons than to the pastor. (Many members view him or her as a "chaplain-outsider who will not be here long. So," they reason, "we need to decide things to suit ourselves.")

Large-church attenders expect to delegate considerable authority to the senior minister, the staff, and the elected and appointed governing-board members. Rather than a participatory democracy that functions through the consensus of all members, large-church attenders expect a representative democracy: "Leadership decisions are taken care of for us by people who know what we should do because they have professional expertise and inside information."

Midsized-church attenders, of course, want both. Some members expect to stamp their approval on all decisions: "Who decided that anyway?" Others expect boards and committees to make decisions. Some members expect the pastor to be a follower: "Where does he think he gets that authority?" Others expect the pastor to be a strong leader: "The pastor needs to take that in hand and tell us what she wants done!"

Procedural differences become especially obvious when a church grows larger or smaller. For similar reasons, pastors who relocate across the invisible boundary lines between size categories often experience role stress (as do many laypersons in the pastor's new congregation). That stress usually lasts eighteen to twenty-four months. During such transitions, pastors (and laypersons whose churches grow larger or smaller) readjust their basic assumptions concerning appropriate procedures for exercising authority and making decisions. The twelve snapshots below illustrate procedural norms in healthy churches of twelve different sizes:

- Churches of 1 to 40 in average worship attendance are like a farmer who employs a seasonal worker to pick apples or grapes (The pastor serves as a supply preacher for Sunday mornings). The speaker meets an appropriate need and has specific "task authority" for preaching. Local residents make all other decisions.
- Churches of 41 to 70 in average worship attendance are like a farm family with several children. Such a church employs outside help for specific tasks such as baling hay or cutting weeds out of the soybeans (The pastor preaches on Sunday, makes hospital calls, buries the dead, and marries the willing). The family delegates to the part-time pastor authority for specific ecclesiastical tasks. Authority for all other decisions is vested in family members.
- Churches of 71 to 100 in average worship attendance are like a "Mom and Pop" grocery store. Part-time or full-time clergy are like the one employee of such a business. They are much appreciated, but they serve more than they lead. The clergy's role is like that of a chaplain.
- Churches of 101 to 300 in average worship attendance are like a YWCA or YMCA. Several specialized programs operate simultaneously, many of which are led by volunteers. Staff lead some of them. The senior pastor's role is like that of a YMCA or YWCA director.
- Churches of 301 to 450 in average worship attendance are like a family-owned business. The family-members/owners (the church members) cooperate with the paid staff to manage various ministries. Staff members equip and serve the standing committees, which retain much of the leadership authority. "Coach" describes the senior pastor's role. The congregation expects him or her to win games by coaching

the staff and lay leaders and by giving symbolic public leadership to the team.

- Churches of 451 to 700 in average worship attendance are like a large department store. Like department heads, the staff lead the committees, providing most of their new ideas. The senior pastor leads the staff in much the same way that a department store manager leads his or her department managers.

- Churches of 701 to 900 in average worship attendance are like a shopping mall containing several privately managed stores. The staff, like individual store owners, not only provide the committees with ideas; they also set their vision and direction. The senior pastor, like the executive of a shopping mall, has control mostly through communicating an overall vision, determining budget processes, and selecting staff wisely (as the mall executive decides who can rent retail space).

- Churches of 901 through 1,800 in average worship attendance are like a publicly owned corporation that values its staff because they bring special expertise to the corporation. Standing committees are fewer, sometimes only three: personnel, finance, and programming. Short-term task forces institute most of the major changes in vision and programming, led by the senior pastor and staff. While lay-governed, the congregation is primarily staff-led. The senior pastor's role is like that of a corporation president.

- Churches of 1,801 to 3,000 in average worship attendance are like a denomination. The sign on the front lawn carries a brand-name denominational label. The congregation sends money home to support its parent, but roles have reversed. The parent needs the child, not vice-versa. The senior pastor is like the CEO of a denomination.

- Churches of 3,001 to 10,000 in average worship attendance are like a medical school. They (a) care for the spiritual needs of attenders, (b) teach other professionals, and (c) publish specialized literature. The senior pastor, often a distinguished writer and speaker, influences not just the staff but also leaders in many other congregations.

- Churches of 10,000 or more in average worship attendance are like a large university with a medical school, a law school, and other schools and departments, each functioning under one organizational umbrella. The senior pastor is like a university president.

Which of these sizes describes your church? Do some of the lay and staff leaders seem to advocate congregational and staff behavior that is one size smaller (or one size larger, if the church has declined in size)? Which books might, if read and discussed in staff or governing board sessions, help speed the church through its stressful transition?[4]

A pastor walking down the hall on Sunday morning stepped into a children's Sunday school class to visit. Fascinated by the plastic church building in which the class collected its offerings, he picked it up. One of the little boys said, "Be careful, John Ed, you have our church in your hands."[5] Such warnings are appropriate every time a church grows larger (or smaller) across one of the twelve unposted lines between church sizes. However, the risk is not limited to the congregation. Pastors and church staff who cross those lines without making behavioral adjustments endanger their own effectiveness and sense of well-being.

7. Property Differences

Small-church attenders expect people to treat the church building as they do their own home, with carefully followed traditions for what rooms are used for, turning off the lights, and tidiness. Large-church attenders expect people to treat the church building like a public institution through which much traffic flows for many different reasons. They do not expect everyone to take good care of the building, and they expect high maintenance costs. Midsized-church attenders have both perceptions, which cause heated discussions in meetings. Some board members want to prohibit use of the building by groups "who do not take care of the building; after all, the church is not for that purpose anyway!" Other board members, many of whom grew up in large churches where thirty or more groups used the building each month and two custodians took care of it, are puzzled by these attitudes.

Where do these differences leave pastors and program staff to whom God has entrusted church leadership? Puzzled, trying to figure out how to make this system work! When they move to a different size congregation (or when their church changes sizes), behaviors honed to precision no longer suit the new circumstances. They must sharpen new behaviors that fit. This takes time, experiences, pain, and determination.

One Size Does Not Fit All

The principal of a private school was trying to understand the stress he was experiencing in his career. Having just completed a doctoral dissertation on the subject of moving from a traditional style of educational leadership to a democratic style, he assumed that these changes were causing his stress. (His research had uncovered many such stresses in other school principals across the United States.)

In conversations with a consultant, the principal realized that much of his stress came from another source: The school had grown from 120 students to more than 500 students in five years. He was still holding himself accountable for giving the kind of personal attention to students and teachers that had worked so well five years ago. Intellectually, he knew this was not possible. Emotionally, his self-identity still depended on those impossible-to-deliver behaviors. He was shooting at an old target, missing it most of the time, and feeling stress and frustration.

Church leaders often recognize similar stresses. Sometimes they blame their stress on the members, the community, or the previous pastor. Sometimes their diagnosis is accurate. At other times the real cause is their own leftover behaviors that fit another size congregation. The good news: The same intelligence that enabled a leader to learn the old behaviors enables him or her to learn new behaviors.

One size does not fit all. Does your behavior pattern fit the size of your present organization or congregation?

CHAPTER 7

WHAT SHAPE
IS YOUR CREATIVITY?

arry was a top-notch salesman. He broke company sales records year after year. Sales trainers cited Larry as an example of perfection. Training manual authors wrote up several of his techniques.

One morning Larry got the news everyone expected: A promotion to regional sales manager. "What a perfect selection!" people said, "Our top salesperson will help increase the sales of everyone in the region." That prophecy did not come true. Larry soon recognized that he was not a top teacher and motivator. He could sell, but he could not articulate the principles behind his successful procedures. Nor was he good at coaching other salespersons. No one thought Larry was a total failure in his new job, but many people recognized that he did not quite fit there.

During the next five years Larry often wished he had his old job back. Then one morning he got a call from the company president in Cleveland. He was being promoted to vice president for new product development. The company CEO saw Larry's years in the field listening to customer needs as perfect preparation for this role. Larry was relieved. He did not look forward to telling his family that they were relocating to Cleveland, but the money would help ease their shock. The new challenge would get him away from a less-than-fun old challenge.

Larry's job in Cleveland was, indeed, better. Yet it did not deliver the satisfaction of his direct selling years. "How can I be two levels up in the company and still feel so dissatisfied?" he thought. "I get to help invent

87

or approve everything our representatives across the world sell every day. But I hate working with concepts and three-year timelines. I am a people person, not a paper pusher."

Larry's journey illustrates that there are three types of leaders, each of which has a different type of creativity: (1) creativity in doing a task, (2) creativity in teaching and coaching the efforts of others who do the task, and (3) creativity at inventing new ways to do the task. Those three types of creativity overlap at some points. Each type of leader, regardless of his or her primary creativity focus, does some of the other two types of work. The three types are not, however, interchangeable. Every organization needs all three types. Think of the tasks involved in building a house, for example. A carpenter, a contractor, and an architect each contribute unique, indispensable skills. By the same token, no one leadership style can replace one or both of the other two. Remove any one of them—doing, teaching/coordinating, or inventing—and the organization's ability to achieve its core objective soon diminishes.

Nor does the personal satisfaction that each kind of leader feels typically transfer when he or she moves to a position that calls for one of the other kinds of creativity. The Person-Environment (P-E) Theory states the obvious: A disparity between the leader's personal preferences and his or her occupational environment generates internal stress.[1] When the individual's needs and abilities match the job's demands and rewards, the P-E fit is good, occupational stress is low, and job satisfaction is high. A poor P-E fit creates the opposite set of leader emotions.[2]

In the field of education, the stress that comes with a poor P-E fit not only affects principals' and teachers' mental and physical health but also detrimentally influences students' cognitive and affective learning.[3] Church consultants frequently see the same kind of stress damaging both the individual leader's personal satisfaction level and a congregation's ministry effectiveness.

- A pastor who accepted a middle-judicatory position was miserable in the job and eventually returned to the local church.
- A young pastor was unhappy in his first church out of seminary. He returned to graduate school, earned a Ph.D., and is happily engaged in seminary teaching.
- A lay staff member became a director of children's ministries for her congregation. A year later she was feeling overwhelmingly stressed by

the details of coordinating teachers and programs. The next year she negotiated a shift to the role of lay pastoral calling, a slot that had opened up when that position's previous occupant moved out of town. As she settled into her new role, the loving contacts made in hospitals and nursing homes gave the former director of children's ministries great satisfaction.

Each of those leaders was intelligent, well trained, energetic, and creative. Each individual, driven by a sense of spiritual calling, a desire to serve, and considerable self-confidence, ended up in the P-E stress that often results from leadership creativity mismatches. Regardless of IQ and other positive attributes, a skilled, creative carpenter (doer) does not necessarily feel satisfaction from working as a contractor (teacher/coordinator) or an architect (inventor).

Unfortunately, no brain scan, blood test, or psychological inventory can adequately predict a leader's P-E fit. Experience, while not a painless teacher of the ministry positions in which clergy and church program staff will reach optimum job effectiveness and personal satisfaction, seems the only teacher available. The early years of ministry help leaders to find their P-E fit. Clergy and church staff who can identify during those initial ministry experiences their leadership creativity type and position themselves in the right slot are doubly blessed: They can spend most of their lives in a role in which they do effective ministry, and they can feel a positive self-identity and high self-esteem while doing that ministry.

An old Arab proverb says that all people are divided into three classes: Those that are immovable, those that are movable, and those that move. Leaders, by definition, influence other people to move (leaders are people with followers). However, leadership happens in a variety of ways, depending on the leader's creativity type. *What shape is your creativity?* Are you a carpenter, a contractor, or an architect?

Carpenters

What church leadership roles require carpenter creativity? Director of volunteer ministries is one. Pastoral counseling is another.

An associate pastor went back to graduate school to obtain specialized training in pastoral care. Excelling in that skill, he graduated at the top of his class. After accepting a staff position at a community pastoral counseling center in Virginia, he developed a fine reputation and a full caseload. Eventually, he became the center's director. That promotion, although it looked like a logical use of his experience and skills, became quite unfulfilling. He hated fund-raising and was not good at it. He did not enjoy managing secretarial staff and coordinating the work of professional staff.

What happened? The counselor's excellent carpenter creativity did not transfer to a contractor creativity role (administration). P-E stress escalated. Family relationships went on the rocks, and a divorce followed. Eventually, he returned to private practice counseling in another city and enjoyed it immensely. His experiences had taught him the shape of his creativity.

Carpenter-creative people are good at carrying out plans and programs. They can continuously perfect a specific ministry skill and use it over a long period without experiencing boredom or burnout. Reliable and dependable, they like the satisfaction of getting things done. They want to enjoy friendly relationships with others while exercising their unique skills or carrying out plans developed by architect types and coordinated by contractor types. They feel comfortable striving for perfection as one spoke of the wheel; they are not energized at the prospect of becoming the wheel's hub or inventing new wheels. They do not enjoy the contractor's role of managing or coordinating the work of other carpenters.

Carpenters enjoy obtaining and applying ideas from books, magazines, and workshops. Carpenters seldom, however, desire to write books or teach others how to use their skills. They want to do something meaningful and worthwhile with their lives. For them that happens by creative application of a specific ministry skill.

Contractors

What church leadership roles require contractor creativity? Director of children's ministries is one. Pastor of a midsized church (101 to 300 average morning worship attendance) is another. Program director in a large congregation is also a contractor job.

A highly respected associate pastor in a midsized church was appointed program director in one of her denomination's megachurches. The job, while paying a bigger salary and viewed as a promotion by colleagues, became an unending nightmare. Coordinating the ministries of eighteen clergy and program staff seemed like herding cats. She developed anxiety-provoked insomnia and began a first-time trip into alcohol over-consumption. That self-prescribed sleep enhancer worked at first, but required increasingly high dosages.

What happened? Her excellent carpenter creativity did not transfer to a contractor-creativity role. At one handhold beyond the end of her rope, she consulted an old friend who suggested an expensive course on "Managing Managers" offered by the business school at the University of Michigan. The church funded her tuition. She absorbed the recommended management principles and came home better equipped to meet her challenges. She never arrived at the hoped-for destination of liking the job as much as she did her previous associate pastor position. But thanks to the specialized management training, she transformed a P-E mismatch into a position from which she derived an acceptable level of satisfaction.

Male chauvinists might believe that this pastor's gender accounted for her transition stress, but research indicates the opposite. Gender may have helped her succeed in this contractor role where a male might have failed. One report that reviewed fifty studies of public-school principals discovered why females are substantially more likely to succeed in such transitions: Female principals tend to lead with a more democratic and less autocratic style than that of male principals.[4] Church observers often note the same contrast between male and female clergy leadership styles.

Why do females often edge out males in contractor creativity jobs? Another study sheds additional light on gender-related differences among persons in supervisory roles:

- Relationships with others are more central to all actions for female administrators than they are for male administrators.
- Teaching and learning is more often the primary focus for female administrators than for male administrators.
- Building community is more often an essential part of the female administrator's style than it is part of the male administrator's style.[5]

Whether they are gender-advantaged (female) or gender-disadvantaged (male), most effective contractor-creative people are good at showing concern and caring. They enjoy being with people. Many of them actually *like* meetings. They see these gatherings as ways to transform energies into results. Contractors excel at handling complex details, which often get clarified and delegated at meetings.

Contractors prefer being liked and accepted, but they are not afraid to risk their popularity by giving the advice necessary to get a task done right. At their professional growing edge, however, many contractors admit that they must counter their own resistance to rapid or unexpected changes in the organization (to them, rapid changes feel like the enemy of smooth, integrated operating procedures). Most contractors also find themselves better skilled at maintaining a program than inventing a new one—a function for which they usually rely on leaders with architect creativity.

Effective contractors fulfill the classic functions of a manager:

- Planning
- Organizing
- Directing
- Staffing
- Controlling

The frequently cited contrast between manager and leader functions is often overstated. All managers do some leading, and all leaders do some managing. But as a general rule, contractors focus more on correctly filling in the details of paint-by-numbers kits than on inventing new pictures. Unlike many of their architect colleagues, they do not neglect the details while looking at the big picture.

One mountaineer said to another, "We almost lost our lives climbing here to the top of Mount Everest to plant the American flag, but it was worth the risk. Hand me the flag."

"I thought you brought it!" his fellow climber replied. This second mountain climber was not a contractor-creative type. That type of person does not forget the flags on the way to the ministry peaks.

Architects

What church leadership roles require architect creativity? The senior pastor of a megachurch is one. The best middle-judicatory bishops are another (mediocre bishops use carpenter creativity, functioning primarily in reactive, rather than proactive ways, a behavior that fits other leadership roles, but not here). The founders of large parachurch organizations are usually architect-creative types (search committees often select a successor with a carpenter or contractor orientation in hopes that he or she will extend the founder's dynasty, which seldom works). Generally speaking, senior pastors of churches whose membership grows rapidly are architect-creative types. In the few exceptions to this generality, an architect-creative associate pastor usually occupies a key staff position.

Joe, senior pastor of a large church, had planted the congregation thirty years ago. Total worship attendance at three morning services now exceeded 2,700. A 5:30 Saturday evening service drew 240. But the last seven years had been less than fun for Joe. The sanctuary was packed and the parking lot capacity maxed out. Even with double Sunday school sessions—9:30 A.M. and 11:00 A.M.—urging people to invite new families to bring their children to Sunday school was unwise: No room at the inn, not even a stable to use for overflow.

In Joe's opinion, the cramped facilities were not the primary ministry lid; attitude was. Strapped with a $3 million mortgage from the last building expansion and landlocked on four acres in a location with little resale value, Joe's lay leaders firmly refused to consider relocation. The seven last words of the church had become a familiar litany in their conversations: "Our church is about the right size!"

This highly skilled senior pastor found himself walking a steep, fast moving, electric treadmill of sermon preparation, luncheon addresses, weekend weddings, and funeral sermons for more than 175 people per year. Joe began feeling like a word factory whose only goal was getting to Sunday lunch and collapsing for a short nap so that he could start again. Burnout became a daily feeling rather than a theoretical buzzword. Like many other successful professionals, Joe was pulling an endless succession of eighty-five-hour workweeks in a high-performance job that helped countless people. But the many redemptive ministries he provided others could not heal the minister himself.

What happened? Joe's feelings of burnout came from a source different from the typical midlife burnout of successful surgeons and psychiatrists. His problem was not simply overwork and the expansion of his role to beyond human capacity. He was an architect-creative pastor trapped in a carpenter-creative role. The P-E match, so perfect in the congregation's early years, became P-E stress when the job no longer fit his kind of ministry creativity.

Seeing no hope of escape except through retirement, he stepped off the treadmill at age sixty. He is presently serving in his fourth interim pastor position—with a congregation that had endured two years of incredible conflict while on the way to firing the previous senior pastor. Joe's other three interim positions had also been with congregations trying to recover from prolonged stress. "I have never had more fun in ministry," Joe says. He is once again meeting major challenges with architect-creative skills.

Most architect-creative people are good at solving problems and creating new programs. Restless and innovative, they are often better at organizing a program than they are at maintaining it. They want to invent and see new ministries accomplished, but they often prefer that others carry the ministries forward into the future. Once they have met the challenge of doing the impossible, doing the routine bores them.

Architects like to grapple with a new challenge, find a solution to it, communicate the solution to others, inspire others to use the solution, and move on to another challenge. Architect-creative leaders differ from contractors and carpenters primarily at the point of their inclination toward and their skill in using intuitive problem solving. While contractors and carpenters are more concerned with applying logic-driven sensory perceptions, architects tend to move against obstacles with imagination-driven intuition. Because they focus less on the details of present ministry paradigms, they often intuitively see the vague outline of a new paradigm before other people know it exists.

That innate ability to look past the present into the future, seeing what others cannot see, makes architect-creative leaders less afraid of failure than their more logic-oriented peers. Concurrent with this capacity comes their greater willingness to move against the tide of public opinion and attempt to reshape public opinion. As Joseph Campbell has said, "It's characteristic of democracy that majority rule is understood as being effective not only in politics but also in thinking. In thinking, of course, the majority is always wrong."[6] Architect-creative leaders, because they see what others cannot see, are willing to challenge majority thinking.

A traveler in Switzerland noticed that the signs at major intersections give the street names little emphasis. (Street names often appear in small letters on the corners of buildings at intersections.) The Swiss place their major emphasis on large, arrow-shaped signs that give the names of towns and point in their direction. The traveler concluded that the Swiss are interested less in knowing where they are than in knowing where they are headed. Architect-creative leaders are much like those Swiss signs. Carpenters and contractors pay attention to present circumstances. Architects are always moving toward the next town.

Are You on the Right Trail?

Cowboys learn how to read signs early in their careers because that skill can help them find strays. Cowboys know, for example, that cattle walking through grass push it down behind them in the direction opposite from where they are headed. A horse pushes the grass forward in the same direction it is moving.

Church leaders guide their lives by attempting to predict whether the jobs they are offered or are inclined to pursue will fit their passions and skills. But such forecasting of ministry effectiveness and personal fulfillment is a far less exact science than what ranchers use to read signs on grassy rangeland. Clergy and program staff are naturally inclined to look at a potential shift in ministry role through the "halo effect" of higher salary, greater prestige, or the opportunity to help more people. In most cases, however, only on-the-job experience tells them what they would have preferred to know in advance. Often, working in a position for one or two years is the only way to learn that glamorous-looking functions and rewards become irrelevant when they possess the kind of creativity that succeeds best in some other type of ministry role.

This is one of the many points at which church leaders must give themselves permission to fail in order to learn. A brief experience in misdirected energy is sometimes the best way to find a trail that fits a particular type of leadership creativity. No matter how well-informed or intelligent leaders become, they sometimes need grace—from God, other people, and self—as they climb the learning curve of discovery. Experience, which always involves the risk of failure, is the primary way church leaders learn the answer to a crucially important question that will strongly influence both their ministry effectiveness and their satisfaction level: What shape is my creativity—carpenter, contractor, or architect?

CHAPTER 8

DOES YOUR PERSONALITY FIT?

I think he is a good choice," the call committee member said as the group discussed a candidate for senior pastor. "He has the kind of personality every pastor needs."

Her professional curiosity aroused, a clinical psychologist serving on the call committee responded, "Say a little more about that. How would you describe the kind of personality every pastor should have?"

"Well, it's hard to put into words," the other committee member replied, "but you know it when you see it. Warm and caring, I guess. Easy to talk to. This man seems a lot like Pastor Jenkins to me. Everyone liked him. He left here seven years ago, and people still talk about him."

Another committee member, the fun-loving church clown and one of the few people who had *not* liked Pastor Jenkins, saw the opening for a joke: "I had a basset hound like that once, but he wasn't good for much. People liked Jenkins, but do you remember the statistical study our committee did? The church's membership declined each of the years he was here. We need strong leadership right now, not just someone who makes good hospital calls."

Conversations of that sort illustrate four important facts: (1) Personality is one of the factors that determines clergy and staff effectiveness. (2) Personality traits are the primary factors church people evaluate when they first meet clergy and church staff. (3) Many church members continue to filter their judgments regarding every other aspect of job performance through the lens of a leader's personality. (4) Personality traits that are effective in one kind of organization or congregation—or at one point in its history—do not always fit different circumstances.

For the past five decades, social scientists have attempted to identify an optimum personality type for religious leaders. No such psychological profile has emerged. One research effort, which reviewed all previous studies of this sort, demonstrated that "psychological evaluation in ministerial selection procedures were unrelated to ratings of job effectiveness."[1] Many denominations use psychological tests as one of the ways to approve or disapprove fitness for ordination. However, none of those instruments accurately predicts future religious leadership effectiveness. Insurance companies have tests that screen out ineffective applicants for sales positions before admitting them to expensive training courses. This is not possible with candidates for clergy and church staff positions.

The conclusions (or lack thereof) drawn from that research seem to contradict common sense and daily observations of reality in congregations and organizations. Every layperson has seen instances in which personality gave a leader the winning or losing edge. Why, then, cannot researchers obtain a psychological profile of the optimum personality for a religious leader? Every pastor and staff member would appreciate knowing whether his or her personality fits the role he or she plays in a congregation or organization. Ordination and call committees could benefit from objective information. With all the sophisticated predictive tests available in other vocations, what explains our ignorance of what the winning edge looks like in ministry roles? The answer to this mystery probably lies in the wide variety of ministry roles and in the extraordinary number of circumstantial and environmental variables in each ministry role equation. Psychologists have not yet identified all of these variables, much less understood their implications.

A review of the research data does, however, highlight four dependable principles that provide clues to this unsolved mystery. Though they do not give us a complete picture of the perfect personality for a religious leader, they help us see why some clergy and staff are more effective than others:

1. Certain personality traits increase effectiveness in some ministry roles.
2. The classic mental health traits increase effectiveness in most ministry roles.

3. Some personality traits reduce effectiveness in most ministry roles.
4. Some highly motivated leaders can modify one or more of their personality traits in order to increase their effectiveness in a specific ministry role.

Do your personality traits fit your ministry position? If so, celebrate. A minute percentage of clergy and staff perfectly fit their ministry roles, especially in the early months and years of their careers. If your personality traits do not fit your ministry role, do not despair. Perhaps you can modify the traits most crucial for effectiveness. If that does not seem possible, perhaps the information in this chapter can help you make decisions regarding the future direction of your ministry career.

Role-Specific Personality Traits

Certain personality traits increase effectiveness in some ministry roles. Take for example, the role of church planter. Denominations risk hefty dollar amounts and future resources when starting congregations. They have therefore sought a picture of the optimum personality pattern for pastor-developers of new churches. Most of their research, using a variety of psychological instruments, points in the same direction.

A ten-year study surveyed sixty-six leading church planters from independent Christian churches using the Personal Profile System, which identifies four basic personality types:

- *D: Dominant Personalities*—driven by tasks and leadership responsibilities
- *I: Influencing Personalities*—driven by people and relationships
- *S: Steady Personalities*—driven by relational and group cohesiveness
- *C: Compliant Personalities*—driven by details and quality-control

This study revealed significant differences in the average worship attendance at churches headed by pastors with these four personality types:

- Churches pastored by high *D* or dominant personalities averaged 181 after 5.2 years.

- Churches pastored by high *I* or influencing personalities averaged 174 after 3.6 years.
- Churches pastored by high *S* or steady personalities averaged 77 after 6.3 years.
- Churches pastored by high *C* or compliant personalities averaged 71 after 4.3 years.

The researchers concluded that, barring unusual circumstances, leading church planter candidates should be high *I*'s, high *D*'s, or a combination of both.[2]

A 1983–1994 study used the Myers-Briggs Type Indicator (MBTI) with 525 church-planter candidates of American Baptist Churches in the U.S.A. During the time of the study, the denomination was making an effort to plant at least 500 new mission congregations. Two Myers-Briggs personality types appeared most frequently among the 525 candidates who wanted to pastor new churches: ESTJ (Extroverted, Sensing, Thinking, Judging) and ESFJ (Extroverted, Sensing, Feeling, Judging). People of both types are solidly grounded in reality; they prefer to work with people and are strongly goal-oriented. The two types differ at one point: How they make decisions.

The T (Thinking) type person is organized and logical. An extreme T person decides to do something because it is efficient, necessary to achieve present goals, or has a positive cost/benefit ratio. *Responsible* is a key descriptive word for the ESTJ type.

The F (Feeling) type person is more value- and feeling-oriented in making decisions. An extreme F person decides to do something because it feels right or has positive ramifications among people about whom he or she cares. *Harmony* is a key description of the ESFJ type.[3]

Later, the study identified from among the 525 church start-up candidates those pastors that went on to plant viable congregations. Eighty-seven percent of the ESFJ types succeeded and 38.5 percent of the ESTJ types succeeded.[4]

Attempts to move beyond that high-definition picture of effective new church planters and find the ideal pastor personality type for congregations of all ages and circumstances have been far less conclusive. A study of 5,200 Southern Baptist pastors revealed that only one-third of the 100 pastors judged by their lay leaders as "truly good" pastors were ESFJ types. The other two-thirds of effective pastors were scattered across the other fifteen Myers-Briggs personality types. The only other common thread: 77 percent of those pastors tested were more feeling oriented (F) than thinking oriented (T).

That study, which also asked lay leaders to identify what distinctive personality characteristics they saw in effective pastors, concluded that church members want their pastors to exhibit three qualities:

1. *Spirituality.* People want a pastor with strong faith, a clear sense of calling, and a high commitment to personal spiritual growth.
2. *Love for people.* Parishioners view extroverts (E) as more effective pastors than introverts (I). This does not mean that introverts (people who draw more energy from being alone than from being with others) cannot pastor effectively; many do. It does indicate, however, that extroverts experience less frustration in their pastoral roles than do their introverted colleagues.
3. *Stability.* Church members, many of whom resist change, like a pastor who supports present traditions and is more geared to meeting current needs than envisioning future possibilities.

Whatever their personality type, effective pastors help people accept change while giving them a sense of stability and continuity. Regardless of their personality type, pastors become less effective when they detach from their congregation either (a) through dictatorial leadership, (b) by insufficient awareness of parishioners' expectations, or (c) by making too many changes too fast.[5]

Does research among new church pastors and clergy in general provide psychological indicators of what the apostle Paul called the gift of pastor (Eph. 4:11)? Probably! Do the traits of effective pastors seem like the same traits we see in Paul, the effective evangelist-apostle? Probably not! Surveys among pastors and laypersons often indicate that they want bishops (middle-judicatory leaders) to serve as "pastors to pastors." However, clergy who are effective in that kind of denominational role, like the apostle Paul, also need envisioning and administrative skills. A particular set of personality traits does not equip a pastor for *every kind* of church leadership role.

The United States mannequin population increases by more than 250 each day. That is almost 100,000 plastic people each year, enough to fill a large sports stadium.[6] Mannequins are practical because their purchasers can use them interchangeably in different stores for different purposes. Fitting clergy and staff members into specific congregations and ministry roles is not like placing mannequins in store window displays. A few leaders can fit two or three different roles with ease, but most cannot. Leaders who early in life find the ministry role into which their personality traits fit are blessed and are a blessing: They experience high levels of personal satisfaction and create similar feelings among the people they lead.

Personality Assets

The classic mental health traits increase effectiveness in most ministry roles. Psychiatric literature carries more precise definitions of insanity than it does of mental health. Concerning mental health, we might say (echoing Justice Potter Stuart's remarks about pornography) that it is impossible to define, but you know it when you see it.[7] Optimum mental health brings with it a positive feeling and behaviors that other people think are healthy. In general, mentally healthy people feel that they possess the twelve classic mental health traits listed below. The degree to which you can affirm the self-assessment statement provided with each trait indicates the level of this mental health trait in your personality.

1. *Strong self-identity.* My positive feelings of self-identity give me a feeling that my life and work is of significant value to others.
2. *Goal orientation.* I have set important future goals for my life.
3. *Hope.* I feel hopeful about my future.
4. *High self-esteem.* My positive feelings of self-esteem strike a healthy balance between self-criticism and self-respect.
5. *Feeling of importance.* I feel recognized, respected, and appreciated by others.
6. *Feeling of being loved.* I feel loved, wanted, and accepted by significant others in my life.
7. *Love for others.* I have opportunities to express feelings of warmth and love toward others.
8. *Stable social relationships.* I feel that I live within a dependable and stable social structure.
9. *Personal freedom.* I feel that I have the personal freedom to make significant life choices.

10. *Opportunities for new experiences.* I have occasional opportunities for the adventure of new experiences that give pleasure to my mind and senses.
11. *Clear personal value system.* My personal value system allows me to handle life's confusing alternatives with relative ease.
12. *Faith in God's providence.* I have a feeling of faith, trust, and mystical relatedness to God and the universe.

The greater the number of these twelve traits that are absent from your life experience, the more you move toward unhappiness and dysfunctionality. If three to five are missing, you probably feel unhappy much of the time. If five to ten are missing, you probably feel that you are bordering on mental illness. If ten to twelve are missing, you are probably under psychiatric treatment, confined due to a mental illness, incarcerated for criminal behavior, or debilitated by substance abuse.

Does the absence of one or more of these twelve mental health traits prevent clergy and staff from becoming effective leaders? No, but such absences create formidable stress, and leaders must expend considerable compensating energy as they try to maintain effectiveness. Does the presence of those twelve mental health traits and the balanced emotional state associated with them make clergy and staff effective leaders? No, but they are definitely assets.

Personality Liabilities

Some personality traits reduce effectiveness in most ministry roles. A study of 123 congregations whose pastors were "involuntarily terminated" revealed that 23 percent of the clergy were seen as contentious, authoritarian, and dictatorial. Another 23 percent were viewed as passive, withdrawn, aloof, uncaring, distant, or cold.[8] Poor mental health can, of course, cause such personality traits. Pastors with negative tendencies can also find them increasing due to dysfunctional dynamics within the organization they serve (43 percent of the churches in the study cited above had internal dynamics that destroyed any possibility of effective pastoral leadership). Regardless of their cause, some personality traits are extreme liabilities in every kind of church leadership role. The following paragraphs discuss the most obvious of those personality liabilities.

Anger/hostility. Everyone feels angry occasionally. That emotion is sometimes appropriate, resulting from abusive statements or actions. Righteous indignation is neither a sin nor a mental abnormality. Chronic, prolonged, unreasonable displays of anger cross over those lines. Hostile outbursts in meetings, a cynicism-laced conversational pattern, habitual fault finding or grumbling, and bringing up old issues at inappropriate times all undermine religious leadership ability. Few potential followers find such expressions of anger attractive. Because many believe that such behavior seems to ignore Jesus' many injunctions to love one another, they look like mismatched clothing on a Christian leader. Then, too, such leaders gradually accumulate a list of people who feel angry at them in return. When that list reaches critical mass, the leader either chooses to leave or is forced out.

People with overly hostile personalities often exhibit several of the following behaviors and emotions:

- irritability over minor experiences
- frequent critical comments to spouse and friends regarding other people
- aggressive tone of voice even when the words are not hostile
- frequent attempts at ego inflation through criticisms of others
- habitually overreacting to suggestions from others
- scolding others in ways that build up protective resentment in the people who overhear
- inclination to "tell people off"

Most hostile people gain considerable benefit from pastoral-care training offered in many seminaries and some large hospitals. Many hostile people find value in the book *How to Get the Most Out of Your Life,* by Paul A. Hauck (Louisville: Westminster/John Knox Press, 1990).

Depression/moodiness. This emotion comes across to others as lack of faith, exactly the reverse of what people expect their religious leaders to project. People with depressive moods often exhibit several of the following behaviors and emotions:

- "a case of the blues" more than two or three days each month
- inability to quickly bounce back from a failure, disappointment, or loss
- disinclination to smile, laugh, or try to amuse others

- physical fatigue
- feeling so "down" that clear thinking and objective judgment are impaired
- feeling that "nobody cares"
- feeling guilty over something done or left undone
- feeling inferior, unloved, lonely, and lacking anything to offer others
- feeling totally blocked from having an essential emotional need met
- feeling of being totally blocked from taking a keenly desired action or life direction
- often feeling ill or complaining about a series of minor ailments
- needing an excessive amount of sleep, or waking up hours too early each day

Many depressed people find that vigorous daily exercise prevents or reduces the intensity of their low feelings. Walking one or two miles each day often generates a more positive mood in three to seven days. However, when the depression does not respond to exercise, it is wise to see a physician. Some depression comes from low thyroid activity or other chemical imbalances in the bloodstream. For many people, brief professional counseling roots out the psychological origins of depression and increases coping skills.

Low social expressiveness, responsiveness, or sympathy. Many individuals with these traits are introverts by nature (drawing their energy more from being alone than from being with others). Often, they have either not recognized the necessity or not perfected the ability to behave in extroverted ways for short periods during public gatherings.

Introverted public behaviors are often interpreted by others as a lack of caring, another trait opposite of what followers expect from spiritual leaders. People with inadequate social expressiveness, responsiveness, and sympathy levels often exhibit the following behaviors and emotions:

- fear of failure in social settings
- timidity and awkwardness when meeting and conversing with new people
- oversensitivity to criticism or teasing
- feeling ineffective in listening and conversation skills
- greeting people with a limp handshake and little enthusiasm or facial animation

- staying silently in the background in a group, waiting for others to initiate communication
- apparent preoccupation with their own internal thought world to the exclusion of others' interests and concerns
- disinclination to show affection or gratitude to others
- apparent boredom or a habit of changing the subject when someone expresses concern about a challenge he or she is facing
- a tendency to treat the strong emotional feelings of other people as irrelevant
- apparent lack of courtesy or sensitivity (introverted people may unintentionally create this impression by not praising people for their success, expressing concern for their pain, or sensing their feelings at high or low times in their lives)
- apparent indifference toward the activities of other sections of their organization or congregation
- failure to appear at social events or meetings where absence sends a signal of disinterest or lack of appreciation
- little expression of interest or concern for the tragedies of other people or groups

Many introverted individuals have low thyroid production or some other chemical imbalance. An appropriate exercise program and a thorough physical checkup are important first steps to countering the effects of these imbalances. A number of people also benefit from training in pastoral care skills offered in seminaries and some large hospitals.

Many leaders who recognize and wish to overcome this liability develop compensatory patterns such as (a) setting up a calendar file that prompts them to remember birthdays or the first anniversary of a spouse's death in order to send a card or make a caring phone call; (b) studying methods outlined in a book such as *How to Talk to Anyone, Anytime, Anywhere* by Larry King and Bill Gilbert (New York: Crown Publishing Group, 1994); (c) methodically making brief appearances at social and organizational events even though they would prefer not to attend; and (d) studying and perfecting responsive listening skills such as those found in books such as *The Caring Church* by Howard W. Stone (Minneapolis: Augsburg Fortress, 1991).

A pastor arriving at a new parish in a small midwestern town pulled up in front of the church building and read the lighted signboard on the lawn.

At the bottom—under the church's name and last Sunday's sermon title—large bold words said, "No Trespassing!" Upon investigation, the new pastor learned that the church had been vandalized on several occasions. Also, many of the community's amorous young couples had been using the back parking lot for other than religious purposes. The frustrated trustees had reacted with the same type of sign a small-business owner would use under similar circumstances.

Pastors and church staff with personality liabilities erect the equivalent of that "No Trespassing!" sign on the front lawn of their leadership. Some personality qualities, although understandable results of genetic heritage and childhood environment, are so incongruous with religious leadership roles that they obliterate a leader's positive skills.

Changeable Personality Traits

Some highly motivated leaders can modify one or more of their personality traits in order to increase their effectiveness in a specific ministry role. Psychological research—derived from personality testing across several decades with the same individuals—indicates that personality traits show little change during their owners' lifetimes. However, history is stacked with examples of great Christian leaders who started with onerous personality traits. As the years unfolded, they modified those traits or harnessed them for specific leadership roles. In some instances, after painful learning experiences and becoming focused in a specific ministry role, their liabilities became assets.

Distinguished historian Albert C. Outler has studied eight truly great evangelists—Paul, Luther, Ignatius of Loyola, George Whitefield, John Wesley, Francis Asbury, Charles Finney, and Billy Graham. Outler pronounced them strikingly similar in psychological makeup: Each one exhibited traits such as aggression, manipulation, and authoritarianism. Wesley, for example, was obsessive-compulsive all his life. His religion did not liquidate that neurotic trait. Wesley also had an authoritarian temper that some of his followers imitated—but without the same results. Outler concluded that in each of the eight personalities, "But for the grace of God and the partial redemption of their power-drives, 'obnoxious' would have been an accurate enough designation of their respective dispositions."[9]

Contemporary studies of clergy indicate that many of them must overcome difficult backgrounds that provided less than positive opportunities for personality development. The Midwest Career Development Service, with offices in Columbus, Ohio, and the Chicago area, assessed 1,359 ordination candidates over a nine-year period. One of the organization's research summaries reports the following:

- 44 percent came from homes regarded as providing a poor emotional climate (neglect or overprotection)
- 13 percent came from families with alcohol problems (a portion of the 44 percent from poor emotional climate homes)
- 13 percent came from homes lacking in geographical roots (also a portion of the 44 percent from poor emotional climate homes)[10]

A well-known athletics axiom says that winning is in your head, not just in your training or prior experiences. Many religious leaders are living proof of that maxim. They grew up in an imperfect environment. Yet through a combination of their sense of spiritual calling and their experiences in ministry, they move from no goals to high goals, from low self-esteem to high self-esteem, and from limited leadership potential to incredible leadership influence.

Leadership Is a Journey

The great good news of the gospel says again and again, "Behold, I make all things new" (Rev. 21:5). Biographies of church leaders repeatedly evidence this truth. People, who are made in the image of God (Gen. 1:27), are free to make choices. They are also free to make new choices. God's spirit often empowers those new choices in ways that build upon but far exceed a leader's personal efforts at lifting themselves up by their bootstraps.

Personality traits are major determinants of leadership effectiveness. They influence whether a leader fits into a particular congregation, organization, or position. What are your personality traits? How could you modify the ones that destroy effectiveness? What could you do to let God modify those traits?

CHAPTER 9

WHAT IS YOUR STYLE?

Rick's nine years followed Gary's seven-year pastorate in a midsized congregation. Both Rick and Gary were well-liked, competent leaders with excellent pulpit and people skills. The church's ministries moved forward in a healthy way during both tenures. However, Rick and Gary conducted remarkably different ministries at several points.

An observant parishioner who liked both pastors said, "They just have different styles."

Unless provided with a questionnaire that forces them to do so, many people who provide references for search committees fail to distinguish between psychological personality traits and personal style. Those two slices of the ministry abilities pie, though similar in some ways, are quite different. Two leaders with excellent personalities that match their roles may use entirely different styles.

As with Rick and Gary, two different styles sometimes fit in the same congregation or organization. In other instances, however, a congregation that responds positively to one leadership style may not feel good about another style.

By the same token, a style that fits in one ministry position may not fit as well in another role. *What style do you exhibit in daily ministry and interactions with colleagues?* Does it fit, sometimes fit, or not fit your congregation or organization?

Are Some Styles Preprogrammed?

The characteristic manner in which clergy and staff meet their needs for emotional security significantly influences their style. A Harvard psychologist, David McClelland, sees people as motivated by one of three basic needs: achievement, affiliation, or power (McClelland uses the word *power* in a morally neutral way).

Achievement. People who are motivated by the need for achievement are concerned less with the rewards of success than with obtaining satisfaction from personal accomplishments. They like to work in positions where they get specific feedback on their efforts. (Some observers feel that fewer clergy operate from this primary drive than from the other two motivations.)

Because these men and women like to see new things happen, they generate much change, especially in programs. An organization can tolerate only so much change in a given time span. When the organization needs a period of stability, these staff members feel far less motivated. They must therefore meet their needs for achievement in some other way—or move to another congregation or position. Some individuals compensate by serving in denominational leadership roles, writing books, or leading community organizations. Many such leaders relocate frequently. A different congregation or position provides greater opportunity to make changes.

Power. People who are motivated by a need for power desire recognition, attention, and the opportunity to exert control over others. Because the question, "Who is in charge?" is important to them, they may work hard to control channels of communication. Revising the organizational structure is another way they make themselves feel more in charge.

People who operate from this internal drive usually get things under their control after occupying a position for several months or years. At that point, they often want to extend their influence to other areas. (Such behavior may or may not be appreciated, depending upon the organization's needs or the emotional drives of other leaders in the system.) Such leaders will carefully ponder the opportunity to relocate. To a great extent, they make their decision to move to a different position or congregation on the basis of whether they think they can exercise control there.

Affiliation. People who are motivated by a need for affiliation desire positive interpersonal relationships, both in groups and in individual friendships. When facing a complex challenge, they are more likely to seek assistance from a friend who is less technically qualified than from an expert with whom they have no prior relationship. This type of leader (the majority of clergy are probably in this category) often does well as a pastor but is not always effective as a program developer or business manager.

Affiliation types like to be with people and feel rewarded as pastoral relationships deepen. Such persons can contentedly stay in one congregation or position for many years. They may resist relocations, despite opportunities for healthy salary increases. "I have all these wonderful relationships," they think. "Is that possible elsewhere? How long would it take to build new ones?"[1]

Which of those three style motivations seems most influential in the choices you make about how to behave and how to spend your time? Did one style influence your decision to relocate or to stay in the same position? Does identifying the primary style by which you meet your needs for emotional security help you understand why you feel fulfilled or unfulfilled in your present ministry role or position?

Role-Specific Styles

Some styles correlate with effectiveness in specific congregations, organizations, positions, and historical circumstances. Four questions can help leaders predict the success or failure of a particular style.

1. *What style feels "normal" to most people in this community's culture?* In many Latin American countries, a "strong-man" leadership style seems normal. In many Asian cultures, a group-consensus leadership style seems normal. In many American communities where blue-collar workers predominate, a more directive leadership style seems normal. In American suburbs comprised primarily of corporate executives and professionals, a leadership style that incorporates considerable involvement from others in the decision-making process seems normal.

This explains why a pastor's style can fit perfectly in one congregation but does not always transfer well to the next pastorate. What is rewarded usually is repeated. But an effective style, practiced so long that it becomes second nature, may be punished in the next church: the right style in the wrong community.

2. *What style feels "normal" to most people in this organization's culture?* Research indicates that style expectations can vary from organi-

zation to organization and among groups within the same organization. Fifty-six percent of the people in one business organization selected "supportive" as the characteristic they most admired in leaders. In another corporation, a majority selected "courage" as the most admired leadership trait. Both organizations were among the best in their respective industries. Yet being helpful and understanding is a key to leadership success in the first one, and the less person-oriented trait of courage is more highly prized in the second one.[2]

The wide variety of "corporate cultures" in religious organizations can also create differing expectations. People are likely to expect a supportive style in James Dobson's leadership of Focus on the Family, and a courageous style in Jesse Jackson's leadership of the Rainbow Coalition. This explains why a church leader's style can fit perfectly in one staff position but not in another: the right style in the wrong organization.

3. *What style feels "normal" to most people who relate to leaders occupying this ministry position?* The same people who are comfortable with a seminary professor's highly directive style (provide structure, exercise control, and supervise) can become irritated when a youth minister uses that style. A large congregation's youth director succeeded because of her coaching style (direct and support). However, she found that same style intimidating when it came from her supervisor, the church's program director. She expected a delegating style from him (give others the day-to-day decision-making responsibilities). An associate pastor who used a supporting style (praise, listen, and facilitate) found that style much less effective when he became the stewardship communicator for a large church: in that role, people expect a technically skilled, directive leader who tells them how to successfully accomplish their task. An elementary school principal in a large church succeeded with a delegating style (give teachers responsibility for day-to-day decision making). She had done far less well as a youth director, where she needed more of a coaching style (direct and support). Using the right style in the wrong ministry position is like planting blueberries in the Sahara Desert.

4. *What style feels "normal" to most people when they expect their church or organization to accomplish a specific set of priorities?* In planting new congregations, for example, a transformational leadership style often gets the expected results—membership growth. A transactional leadership style, which most people in established churches view as quite appropriate, seldom produces the increases in membership and

worship attendance essential to a new congregation's viability.[3] Few parishioners have read that research, but they can recognize the two styles.

A transformational leader usually exhibits the following traits: charisma; intellect; individual consideration for followers; clear definition of the organization's basic purpose; and the ability to envision and communicate a desired future that a critical mass of followers accept. A transformational leader often changes what is considered appropriate for discussion; changes organizational self-identity, beliefs, authority systems, work norms and behaviors; and invents new cultural forms.

A transactional leader usually accepts and works with the present organizational culture; accepts what can be talked about; accepts and maintains present organizational self-identities, authority systems, beliefs, work norms and behaviors; and uses the organization's present rituals, stories, and role models to communicate its values.[4]

The title of a speech given at a college alumni banquet raised this question: "What should you do if you do not have charisma?" One of the banquet attenders whispered to another a profound truth, "Thank God, and feel fortunate." One style does not fit all congregations or organizations. Leaders in some circumstances and positions need charisma. In other settings, followers punish rather than reward charisma.

Several people died when a small private plane crashed into a large commuter plane as both attempted to take off. The news service quoted someone as saying, "Receiving a license to fly a small plane after a few hours of training is like giving someone a license to learn." People with seminary degrees or church staff positions are not as dangerous as inadequately trained pilots, but their roles are more like a license to learn than a destination. Effective leaders gradually become conscious of their personal style; understand what style fits in a congregation, organization, position, and set of historical circumstances; and modify their style to fit, or find another position where it does fit.

Universally Effective Styles

Some leadership styles are role-specific, but several style traits seem to work well in all congregations, organizations, and circumstances. Among those universally positive style traits, the following are especially obvious.

1. *Spiritual Consciousness.* All effective religious leaders illustrate through their words and behaviors that God is the origin and destination

of their endeavors. This style usually includes an emphasis on prayer, Bible study, and worship. This leadership focus reminds people that rational thinking is important but not enough by itself; organizational procedures are important but not enough by themselves.

In the Middle Ages, being knighted gave someone a special relationship with the king. Knights therefore exhibited a value system and level of consciousness that set them apart from other citizens. Effective Christian leaders, because they have been "Christed," are living signposts whose words and behaviors point people toward God. A spiritually conscious style is an observable, powerful addition to whatever other leadership skills you bring to a ministry role.

2. *Enthusiasm.* Meaningful ideas delivered in a dull, listless manner can seem irrelevant. The same ideas, communicated with enthusiasm, can light the fire of commitment that leads to positive change.

A few of society's roles require a low enthusiasm level. We do not expect morticians, for example, to exhibit high enthusiasm for their work. Enthusiasm adds value to most other roles, especially those related to "intangible" products such as Christianity.

3. *Joyful Attitude.* Blended with enthusiasm, a joyful spirit draws people toward a leader's goals as dependably as the moon pulls the tides. This happens in three principal ways: First, joyfulness counterbalances the ever present temptation to take oneself too seriously, a behavior that repels rather than attracts followers. Second, joyfulness and a sense of humor help people relax and enjoy their work more. Third, joyfulness sends the signal that a leader values followers so much that having fun as they work together is as important as the work itself. Along with its positive influence on the leader's ability to lead, a sense of humor increases a group's creativity and thus the quality of its work.

Homiletics guru Fred Craddock told in a sermon of his airport conversation with a surgeon from the University of Utrecht in Holland. The surgeon told Craddock that the conversation between doctors and nurses while the patient is under anesthesia influences the patient's mood in the recovery room. If the doctors and nurses are gloomy, grim, critical, and negative during surgery, the patient will for reasons unknown to the patient wake up feeling depressed and despondent. If the doctors and nurses are jovial and cheerful, the postoperative patient is euphoric, happy, and optimistic. After sharing this with Craddock, the Swedish physician asked Craddock if he was a surgeon. Craddock replied that he was a preacher, but added that if it worked in surgery it would work in the sanctuary.[5] A joyful attitude produces positive results everywhere in the congregation and in every kind of church organization. This powerful style enhances whatever other leadership skills people bring to a ministry role.

4. *Spiritual Optimism.* The Bible calls this hope. People who dispense the quality of hope in their conversational patterns are appreciated like the first rain after a long drought. They attract allegiance to themselves and their goals. As Colin Powell put it, "Perpetual optimism is a force multiplier."[6]

The early DC-3 passenger planes had a tail wheel, and the aisle slanted down toward the back of the plane. One mischievous pilot often carried a handful of nuts and bolts in his flight bag. As the plane revved up and started down the runway, he would reach around the cockpit door and throw several nuts and bolts into the aisle—where they rattled and rolled their way toward the back of the plane. This kind of humor did not inspire confidence in the passengers and was frowned upon by airline officials.

Church people feel like the passengers on this pilot's plane when they encounter chronic pessimism in spiritual leaders. As one regional denominational executive said, "If you have depressive feelings about the future, you cannot lead." Another executive advises pastors to take their problems to God and their faith to the people. A successful fund-raiser for church building expansions says that one of the ways he decides whether he is willing to lead a church's campaign is by asking the pastor, "Do you believe it will happen?" The fund-raiser then watches the pastor's eyes and body language.

Lack of optimism can damage every other church endeavor. Conversely, possession of this powerful style enhances every other leadership skill people bring to a ministry role.

5. *High Energy Level.* Most effective leaders have the stamina to maintain a fast pace and juggle several demands simultaneously. Often, their work involves long hours, about which they seldom complain. Most of them agree with Lewis Carroll's observation in *Alice in Wonderland*: "It takes all the running you can do to keep in the same place. If you want to get somewhere else, you must run at least twice as fast." The presence or absence of a high energy level advances or retards every other leadership skill people bring to their ministry roles.

6. *Self-discipline.* Some people accomplish two to six times as much as do their coworkers during the same forty-hour week. Such incredible

productivity usually comes from a high energy level supercharged by motivation and self-discipline. Taken too far, that style becomes obsessive-compulsive behavior, often accompanied by some abrasiveness and a lack of people skills. However, without self-discipline, one tends to become apathetic or drift into the future with oars still in the locks. Self-discipline enhances every other leadership skill people bring to their ministry roles.

7. *Positive Appearance.* Neat apparel, shined shoes, and well-kept hair do not bring people into the kingdom of God. But if the package is shabby people may not bother to examine its contents. Positive appearance enhances every other quality people bring to a ministry role.

8. *Tactfulness.* Effective leaders know the difference between what could be said and what should be said. Their minds and tongues are sufficiently Velcro-connected to stop most of the unnecessary "could-be-saids" from becoming audible.

Someone described a well-educated but tactless pastor as "more interested in ideas than in people." Competent religious leaders understand the difference between telling the truth and telling the truth all the time, in situations and to people with whom it accomplishes no practical purpose. Competent leaders know that a lack of tact can debilitate every other positive quality they bring to their ministry roles.

9. *Flexibility.* The initial response of effective leaders to new ideas from others often conveys a "Why not?" attitude. The leader then asks questions, listens, and asks follow-up questions, trying to get every possible aspect of the new idea out on the table. Less effective leaders tend to immediately put up barriers to a new idea by citing several reasons why it will not work. Later, they may feel they were too hasty, and come back to the idea giver with a more open attitude. By that time, however, the person who offered the idea may feel far less enthusiastic. A leader's eventual flexibility cannot compensate for initial rigidity that usually makes people feel rejected, stymied, or stupid.

Flexible leaders combine firm convictions with the ability to hear and discuss dissenting viewpoints in meetings and conversations. Often willing to experiment with a suggestion until it is proved or disproved, capable leaders concentrate more on deepening relationships with their followers than on maintaining arbitrary rules about administrative details. Integrity and flexibility help them strike a balance between rigidity and anarchic chaos.

10. *Conviction Without Dominance.* An overcontrolling, dominating style, usually learned from childhood parental models, is sometimes inextricably linked to inflexibility. Leaders with this style tend to come on strong in meetings, seem sure of themselves and their opinions, and are fond of trying to convert others. To check your dominance quotient, ask whether any of the following items describe you:

- When in a hurry, I sometimes order people to do things instead of asking them for help.
- I often go after what I want with firm determination, not learning until later that I failed to take into account someone else's feelings.
- I often find myself arguing with someone over matters that seem inconsequential.
- I often feel that I need to stand up for my rights or fight for a principle.
- As a child, I had to take a great deal of responsibility at an early age.
- I grew up with a dominating, overcontrolling parent, elder sibling, or other authority figure.

Highly dominant people sometimes excel as military officers or business executives. When this style is buffered by other, more beneficial traits, such individuals sometimes rise to top offices in religious organizations. In some cases, especially if their role is sharply defined into a compartment such as teaching, writing, or public speaking, their immediate subordinates may be the only people who feel stressed by their dominance. If, however, their ministry role requires considerable interaction with people, such leaders usually find themselves either working hard to compensate for their inflexible, dominant style, or working to find a leadership position where it fits better.

11. *Indiscriminate Affirmation.* Effective leaders intuitively understand that the best form of constructive criticism is praise. Despite a truckload of logical reasons to criticize or complain, their conversational patterns are full of praise. They may never have read some old often-quoted business research statistic which claimed that most employees consider themselves above average (75 percent of all employees rate their abilities in the top 25 percent of people in their field, according to that), but effective leaders instinctively communicate from that understanding of human nature.

When three-fourths of people think their performance is in the upper one-fourth of their peers, even the absence of praise can feel like criticism. Consequently, effective leaders do not merely restrain themselves from criticism when things go wrong; they do not remain silent when things go right (or seem about average).

12. *Nonjudgmental Attitude.* Effective leaders communicate grace (psychological acceptance) to people who do not possess moral, ethical, or religious standards identical to their own. They understand that the habit of analyzing and criticizing may be appropriate for a quality-control inspector on an assembly line but works well in few other places. They also understand that what lives in the heart eventually seeps into the conversation. Therefore, they avoid dwelling on negative thoughts about other people.

13. *Forgiving Spirit.* Effective leaders understand that a poor memory of the ways in which others have injured them is one of the golden keys to positive personal and group relationships. Jesus washed his disciple's feet and told them to do likewise. Jesus was illustrating in this active parable that loving others goes far beyond a generalized, positive attitude. Love means washing the feet of people who do not deserve it, have done wrong, have done you wrong, or have produced less than their best effort in your organization's ministry. This includes forgiving people who do not deserve it (as Jesus washed his feet, Peter was about to deny he ever knew Jesus). This includes forgiving people who have not yet requested it.

14. *Balance.* Effective leaders pay attention to numerous responsibilities rather than riding one hobbyhorse (and justifying their behavior by remarking that the other duties will take care of themselves if the leader focuses on this one item). Capable leaders know that hobbyhorse riders usually generate much activity accompanied by little forward movement.

Commitment, Skill, and Efficiency Are Not Enough!

Effective pastoral and church staff leadership requires a combination of many factors, each of which is important. Style increases or reduces the brightness of each star in that leadership constellation. When a leader's style does not fit a ministry role or congregation, he or she can become a meteor that gets attention briefly while burning out.

"Give me the right teachers, and everything else will follow; give me the wrong teachers, and nothing else matters," James Bryant Conant is reported to have said when he was president at Harvard University.[7] Those words apply to many kinds of organizations, especially churches. The leaders are the program. The right person with the right skills and the *right style* often makes more difference in the outcome of a ministry than do the best of facilities and a bank full of money.

A tourist on a German autobahn was buzzing along at more than 140 kilometers per hour with his map laid across the steering wheel. Apparently unable to see the speedometer, he was passing everyone. However, he was doing something that few church leaders can overdo: trying to get a fix on where he was and in what direction he was heading.

Too often, the pressure of daily details encourages leaders to concentrate only on speed and efficiency. In religious leadership, a map and a compass are as important as a speedometer. Figuring out whether your style fits your location and where this style will probably take you is a highly influential leadership factor. What does your map say?

CHAPTER 10

Do Your Clock Habits
Achieve Your Goals?

A denomination published its annual activities calendar with thirty-one days in both June and November (months that only have thirty days). One church leader identified that printing error as a Freudian slip. Would not every servant of God wish to add some days to the year?

Since that is not possible, the only alternative is better management of the standard 365-day model. For most leaders, however, that too seems like a formidable challenge: time management is simultaneously their greatest need and a problem about which they are certain that nothing can be done.

The term *time management* seems like an oxymoron to most church leaders—two words that make no sense when linked together. But meeting the challenge of time management, which sometimes seems as hopeless as mud-wrestling an alligator, is not impossible. Several effective principles and methods have emerged in recent years. Some of these come from the business world; others are unique to church life. As you review the thirty-six characteristic thinking and behavior patterns of effective religious leaders listed below, ask yourself the following questions: *Do my clock management habits help or hinder my productivity in my congregation or ministry position?* Which of these principles am I already using? Which ones could I consider using?

1. *Good clock managers believe God requires them to manage their time.* The way we spend our time is the way we spend our life. That makes

time management a theological matter, not just a methodological consideration. The apostle Paul tells us, "Moreover it is required of stewards that they be found trustworthy" (1 Cor. 4:2). Time does not belong to us. It belongs to God. If we view our time as a spiritual resource, we will seek to be good stewards by learning and applying effective time-management techniques. If we do not see time that way, we will continue to let circumstances manage our lives.

2. *Good clock managers understand that time use determines ministry effectiveness.* Church leaders work with five resources: time, people, money, buildings, and equipment. Of these five, time is the hardest to manage because we cannot see it. Yet this invisible resource determines what we accomplish with the other four.

3. *Good clock managers understand that they have all the time they need to do God's will for their lives.* Christ died at age thirty-three—younger than most people reading this page. Yet some of Jesus' closing words were, "It is finished" (John 19:30). Can you imagine a God who is so unfair that he would give you a job to do and then refuse to give you the time in which to do it? When you find yourself constantly running out of time, one or both of two things is happening: either you are doing things that are not God's will for you to do with your life and gifts, or you are doing God's will in an inefficient manner.

4. *Good clock managers understand that if they do not take charge of their time other people will take charge of it for them.* People are standing in line to take charge of every leader's time. If you neglect the responsibility of time management, others will handle it. What if your personality is so passive—or your need to be liked is so great—that you are willing to let other people determine your focus for you? If that is the case, no amount of exposure to good time-management methods will help. You have delegated to others something for which you and you alone are responsible.

5. *Good clock managers know that they are never powerless over time problems.* We all experience stressful periods in which all we can do is try to keep afloat in a sea of demands. But over the long haul, each of us can take control of our time and our life if we desire to do so. To pretend that we cannot is one or both of two types of theological denial. We are either denying the free will God has given each of us or denying our responsibility and accountability for the stewardship of life and gifts God has given us. Usually, the answer consists of equal amounts of both types of denial.

6. *Good clock managers do not confuse busyness with effectiveness.* Several factors encourage leaders to idolize activity: a parade of school teachers telling us to "get busy"; years of trying to look busy when the boss is around; years of hearing about successful, *busy* executives. Yet the world seldom proclaims an accomplishment good just because it took a lot of time. Good time managers do not confuse activity with results.

7. *Good clock managers do not confuse long hours with effectiveness.* Most full-time religious leaders experience a longer-than-average work-week. For example, studies in the early 1960s reported an average workweek for pastoral ministers of sixty-four hours. Studies in the 1980s and 1990s reported similar results. Yet there is no real correlation between long hours and effectiveness. Good time management lies in a totally different direction; it involves choosing very carefully what we do with the hours we have.

8. *Good clock managers do not confuse efficiency with effectiveness.* In footraces in ancient Greece, the winner was not the runner who attained the finish line first but the one who crossed in the least time with his torch still burning. Efficient people get their work done quickly. Effective people get the right work done—which sometimes means they leave completely undone some work they could have done efficiently and quickly.

9. *Good clock managers can tell the difference between important work and essential work.* All essential work is important, but not all important work is essential. For a pastor, some of the essential work is preaching and hospital calling. Much of the other work is important but not essential. The list of essential work will change somewhat each time a pastor moves to a different parish or leadership position. Make a list of essential tasks and review the list at least annually. Otherwise, the many important items that claw at your door and telephone daily will soon take charge of your time.

10. *Good clock managers are goal-driven rather than time-driven.* Time management is a process of reaching stated goals by effectively using the least amount of time. We reflexively tend to begin at the wrong end of that definition—trying to shrink our expenditure of time. That is usually a mistake. Time management may be a bad term. Perhaps we should call it goal management. That is where good time management begins—deciding on the goals we want to reach by the use of our time.

Until we are clear about our goals, we cannot be clear about how to use our time. If we shoot at nothing, we usually hit it. But if we shoot at the wrong target, hitting it does not matter. Therefore, deciding precisely what gifts God has given you and how he is calling you to use those gifts—then separating those from the many other things you know you could do or other people think you ought to do—is the bottom line of time management. Dedicate yourself to doing forty good things, and you will soon be unable to do any one of them exceptionally well. Ministry requires flexibility and the ability to juggle multifaceted responsibilities. But effective ministry also requires focus. A river without banks is a swamp.

11. *Good clock managers have specific plans on paper for how to achieve their goals.* High ideals and fine goals need landing gear as well as wings. Without concrete plans, what tends to happen is nothing—in large quantities. Good time managers (high achievers) tend to put their plans on paper, periodically updating them in light of changing circumstances. Poor time managers (low achievers) drift into the future like a nomad without a compass in the desert, hoping to accidentally find a green oasis.

12. *Good clock managers are highly aware of how they use their time.* After you set clear ministry goals and make plans for how to reach them, you can analyze your time expectations in terms of those goals and plans. Find out what matches and what does not. Ask yourself why you are doing activities that do not fit your goals and plans. What would happen if you did not do them? If the answer is nothing, stop doing them.

To become more aware of how you use your time, chart your behavior for four weeks on a daily and hourly time log, using fifteen-minute segments. This gives you a reality base from which to reorganize your time so that it supports your long-term ministry goals. A one-month time log will accomplish three things: First, it will identify who and what causes most of your interruptions. Second, it will identify especially time-consuming tasks that you should delegate to other people. Third, it will identify several unscheduled activities that you should relocate into specific time blocks each week. You cannot use your time more wisely (to match your goals) until you know how you presently use it.

13. *Good clock managers identify and chop out time wasters that do not fit with their essential work, goals, and plans.* People in widely

differing types of work report the same kinds of time wasters. Forty colonels and commanders at the Canadian Forces School of Management in Montreal constructed the same list of time wasters as did thirty college presidents in the midwestern United States. Salesmen from a large insurance company named time wasters similar to those identified by the leaders of black religious organizations. When asked to identify their time wasters, managers invariably list external causes first, such as telephone calls, meetings, visitors, paperwork, and delays. After they discuss some time-management principles, managers usually discover a list of internal time wasters, such as lack of delegation, lack of plans and priorities, procrastination, and the open door policy.[1]

Which of your time wasters are generated externally (by events or other people)? Which time wasters are generated internally (by your own behavior and attitudes)? Good time managers do more than manage time. They must manage themselves.

14. *Good clock managers use zero-based time management.* Barnacles are little organisms that grow on the hulls of ships. As time passes, barnacles accumulate and begin to cause a drag on the ship's progress through the water. (This is why ships must occasionally be put into dry dock—to have the barnacles cleaned off their hulls.) Every religious leader discovers that time barnacles grow on the hull of his or her ministry. These cause a creeping loss of time control as a leader develops new projects and programs. For many leaders, that accumulation starts in the fall and builds through the year.

Each August, as a part of your personal devotion time, do zero-based time management. List all the things you do each month. After two or three days, come back to the list and ask yourself which items are essential. Which items could other people do, if you gave them the proper opportunity and training? Once you make these decisions, list the people to whom you could delegate these responsibilities. Then do it.

Repeat this zero-based time management process each summer. Life is a continuous process of change. You will never finish the process, but the time you spend deciding how to use your time is one of the best time expenditures you can make.

15. *Good clock managers have a high awareness of personal strengths, limitations, and drives.* Your psychological makeup greatly influences your willingness and ability to make good use of your time.

- Highly anxious people have difficulty managing their time. The higher their anxiety level, the greater their difficulty in concentrating on and implementing a consistent plan.
- Constant feelings of mild depression undermine good time management. The more depressed people are, the more they have difficulty concentrating.
- Strong relational needs that often accompany gregariousness can "eat up" time. Pastors, for example, have several responsibilities that they can accomplish only when they are alone. One of those is preparing sermons.
- A high need for recognition can decrease time-management ability, because it can cause people to say yes to more requests than they can accommodate.

The way psychological factors play out in leaders' thoughts and emotions greatly influences whether they use or do not use effective time-management methods.

16. *Good clock managers concentrate on using their strongest talents rather than on trying to prop up their weak skills.* Try to discover your personal gifts for ministry and use them as much as possible. God has given them to you for a purpose. If you are a pastor, for example, you must do at least nine different things, and you usually do two or three of them really well. Unless they are on your list of essentials, try to delegate tasks that call for your less-developed skills to someone who has those gifts. If an item that calls for your less-developed skills is on your essentials list, try to learn how to do it better (if you can increase your skill slightly, you will spend less time on the task and have more hours available for tasks that use your primary gifts). Do not waste your life feeling guilty about what you cannot do well. Go with the flow of your strengths. Only God is good at everything.

17. *Good clock managers set deadlines on paper for accomplishing major tasks.* Creative juices flow best when you work against deadlines (for some people, that is the only time the juices flow). After you decide on a goal, your next reflexive thought should be to "when it." Ask yourself

when you are going to achieve the goal. If it is a small item, do it immediately. If it is a larger, more complex item, decide on your target time for having it done.

18. *Good clock managers use "to do" lists.* Lists help leaders in two major ways: (a) Lists reduce worry and improve concentration, allowing you to stop fretting about a project because you know having it written on paper will protect you from forgetting it. (b) Lists create a consistent reminder because you see an item every day until it is done.

19. *Good clock managers plan their time in weeks and blocks, not in hours or days or minutes.* Set up a sheet with twenty-one time blocks—morning, afternoon, and evening for each of the seven days of the week. (This does not replace the weekly calendar on which you put appointments; that is another matter.) Set aside all three blocks on one day for a day off. That leaves eighteen blocks. Assign two additional blocks to leisure and family. That leaves sixteen blocks. If you are a senior pastor, plug in the appropriate number of blocks for sermon preparation and hospital visitation. Many pastors also designate one evening block each week for visiting unchurched persons (perhaps Monday) and another evening for visiting members (perhaps Tuesday).

Some pastors ask each church staff member to share his or her planning guide with other staff members at each weekly staff meeting. This helps everyone hold one another accountable and ensures that staff members' families are not deleted from the clergy concern list.

20. *Good clock managers develop the ability to concentrate on one task at a time.* "Bracketing" is the skill of focusing on one specific item at a time, rather than jumping around from task to task like a fly in a candy shop. What if a stray thought regarding some other important task interrupts your concentration? Write it down on a piece of paper or a "to do" list and return your attention to the task you have bracketed for the moment.

21. *Good clock managers use their most productive hours of each day for prime projects that require creativity and clear thinking.* Leaders, like everyone else, have different circadian rhythms (physiological patterns that cause people to peak in energy, thinking ability, and brain function at certain times of the day). No amount of willpower changes that system. For many leaders, prime time is in the morning hours; for others, afternoons allow the best creative thinking.

22. *Good clock managers expect interruptions but do not let every interruption control them.* Interruptions are sometimes irritations and sometimes opportunities. Sometimes they are both, and sometimes we cannot judge which they are in the beginning. We are tempted to lock ourselves into our schedules and never come out for any reason. That kind of compulsive inflexibility is dangerous.

Interruptions are part of every leader's job. You must push back a deadline on an important project if something essential interrupts you. But make sure that you set priorities in ways that allow you to distinguish between essential interruptions and important interruptions (as in football, you tackle the guy who comes through the line carrying the little brown ball. You do not tackle everybody who comes through the line.)

23. *Good clock managers learn how to say no graciously.* Anyone who sets clear goals and priorities must inevitably say no to some requests. If we say yes to everything, we are letting other people set our goals and reorganize our priorities.

Because church leaders have answered the call to enter a profession in which they are supposed to help people, their minds easily become set in a yes mode. Saying no does not feel right. Unfortunately, however, saying yes to enough things means you will eventually have to say no to something.

Prostitutes say yes to everyone. Monogamous marriage partners say yes on a far more selective basis. In both time management and marriage, the end result of saying yes to everyone is disastrous.

24. *Good clock managers do not try to remember anything.* Anything you really intend to do requires one of two actions: Either do it at this moment or write it down. Most people are under the illusion that they can remember what someone tells them and what they promise people they will do. That assumption is only partially accurate. Memory systems are quite fallible, and a leader's credibility is eventually damaged when he or she forgets that a parishioner is hospitalized or lets a promise to put something in the church newsletter fall through the cracks of a busy week. The following four-point system allows you to handle countless details without having to remember anything:

- Carry a small notebook in your pocket or purse. If you decide to take care of something next week, do not rely on your ability to remember it. Write it on a page in your notebook. (Do not make lists. Put a new item on each page.)

- When you arrive at the office each morning, tear out the notes and place them in action stacks on your desktop—phone calls to make, letters to dictate, and so on. Between interruptions, try to complete these action stacks by the end of the day.

- Empty one of your desk drawers and designate it your "holding drawer." Put in this drawer items that you cannot do this week because you are waiting for someone to call or write with the information you need. Every Monday morning, open the holding drawer and look at each sheet of paper. Some matters have now reached the crisis stage. You must telephone someone and get the information this week, before it is too late. Other items can wait another week or more, so you put them back in the drawer.

- Set up a monthly calendar file (some people call this a "tickler file"). Whatever you call it, label twelve file folders with the twelve months of the year and put them in a nearby file cabinet. On the first day of each month, pull its folder, dump onto your desk all the reminders you have put in the folder, and take appropriate action on them.

These four methods work together in a synergistic way that releases you from the pressure of having to remember everything. If you plan to do something, write it down and put it into the flow of this four-point system. Work on the action stacks on your desk daily, so they do not accumulate. Open the holding drawer weekly. Open the calendar file monthly. The results: Your anxiety (and guilt) about forgetting things will drop. You will develop a reputation as a dependable, capable person who gets things done.

25. *Good clock managers learn how to delegate.* Delegation is one of the hardest management skills to learn. Nobody is born with it, and our childhood training equips us for doing things ourselves rather than delegating them to others. Most people do not, therefore, learn how to delegate unless forced into it.

Several kinds of psychological hangups keep people from delegating effectively. The most common hangup is perfectionism, accompanied by the feeling that "nobody can do this quite as well as I can do it." Another hangup is the fear of giving away power and authority. Another is the sense of security that many people find in doing detail work (when they quit working on details, they begin feeling insecure and unconsciously seek more details to work on).

Good delegators convince themselves that other people can do a job well if given sufficient time, training, and authority. As the delegator gains experience, he or she learns that delegating is a ministry. When people succeed at the responsibilities delegated to them, their self-esteem increases. An effective delegator enables other people to experience the same joy, achievement, and creativity that he or she likes to experience.

26. *Good clock managers are concerned about everything, but they avoid taking responsibility for the details of everything.* Concern for people and projects is one aspect of being a Christian. Taking responsibility for everything in the church or organization is acting like a football quarterback who tries to play all the positions.

After you complete your horizontal delegation to other people, a few items remain that neither you nor other people can handle. Delegate these to God. Leaders who do not learn vertical delegation will have a driven, ineffectual ministry, and some of them will suffer emotional breakdowns.

27. *Good clock managers who have secretaries learn to use a dictating machine.* In addition to letters, dictate filing assignments and other projects to your secretary and memos to staff members. This can save countless hours of conversations with a secretary—a procedure that eats up time for two people, not just one.

28. *Good clock managers handle their mail only once.* Some leaders open their mail, glance at it, and lay it on the desk. They come back the next day and look at it again, trying to decide what to do with it. Some people look at their mail four or five times.

Take one of four actions with every piece of mail:

- Read it and throw it away.
- File it or dictate instructions that enable your secretary to file it for you.
- Take action on it immediately, or put it in one of the action stacks on your desk.
- Put it in the "take action tomorrow" stack on your desk (some mail is complicated, and you need to think about it overnight before responding). By tomorrow, decide what to do with the item—dictate a letter, file it, put it in the holding drawer or calendar file, or some other action.

People who handle mail several times and decide not to decide what action to take have decided one thing: They are willing to waste precious ministry hours.

29. *Good clock managers have a filing system that is a good finding system.* For example, one filing system that works well in congregations uses file folders with tabs on the left side, in the middle, and on the right side. Each type of folder has a differently colored label. Left might be red; middle, blue; and right, green. Use the left-hand files for major headings such as administration, Christian education, and stewardship. Use the middle files for information relating to different aspects of the major headings. Use the right-hand files for subheadings of the middle files. For example, a left-hand file labeled "Christian Education" would hold materials relating to the broad topic of Christian education. Behind this file might be several middle files such as "Children," "Senior Adults," "Young Adults," "Youth," and so on. Behind the middle file labeled "Youth" there might be two right-hand files labeled "Junior High" and "Senior High."

Every church's headings, subheadings, and sub-subheadings will be different, especially the subheadings and sub-subheadings. As you evaluate your role and your church's needs you will be able to adapt this filing system to fit your congregation; but listed below are several headings that should appear in most churches' filing cabinets.

MAJOR HEADINGS *(left-hand file)*	**SUBHEADINGS** *(middle file)*	**SUB-SUBHEADINGS** *(right-hand file)*
Administration	Calendar Files (twelve separate file folders labeled for each month of the year). Constitution and Bylaws Board Meetings	
Christian Education	Audiovisual Catalogs Youth Work	Junior High Senior High
Community Agencies	Habitat for Humanity	

(left-hand file)	(middle file)	(right-hand file)
	Drug Treatment Centers	
Denominational Work	District Work	
		Youth Council
	National Work	
	Regional Work	
Evangelism	Calling Methods	
Homiletics	Special Day Sermon Ideas	
Ministry	Health Insurance	
	Pastoral Relations Committee	
Membership Development	Current Membership Lists	
Missions	Burma Mission Hospital	
Pastoral Care	Alcoholism	
	Depression	
Property	Purchasing Information	
Public Relations	Press Release Forms	
Stewardship Materials	Wills	
Worship		Christmas Programs and Materials
		Special Days and Services

In a well-organized file system, finding something is easy. You can usually think of what major category (left file) the item that you are hunting fits into. After defining your search into that general area, finding the item in a subheading or sub-subheading file is easy.

30. *Good clock managers are decisive.* People who pick up letters or projects six times over several weeks and lay them back on their desks as

they try to decide how to handle them do double damage: They steal time from other purposeful activities, and they reduce the likelihood of success in their profession and projects.

This destructive habit arises from several sources. Some people's indecisiveness is simply one aspect of a passive personality. Other people fail to decide because of their low energy level. Still others avoid decisions because they suffer from chronic procrastination—the habit of turning matters over and over in their minds for days, weeks, or months. Many procrastinators are secretly perfectionists who are afraid to decide because the result might not be perfect. Some procrastinators grew up in families in which extreme wrath descended on them when they made decisions for themselves (so for them, not deciding is an emotional defense mechanism).

Adopt the habit of doing one of three things within twenty-four hours after something comes to your desk: Do it, delegate it, or drop it.

- Decide that it needs to be done and that you and you alone can do it. Do it immediately or put it on your "to do" list or in your holding file for action as soon as possible.
- Decide that it needs to be done and someone else can do it. Delegate it to that person. (The higher on the management ladder you get, the more items you must decide in this way. Otherwise, you will not have time to effectively do what you and you alone can do.)
- Decide that it does not fit in your system of goals and priorities. Drop it.

When you have made a good decision but made it too late, you have decided badly by not deciding. A bad decision is almost always a better risk than no decision at all.

31. *Good clock managers control telephone time leaks.* There are many actions you can take to improve telephone communication and save time.

Before you make a call, jot down the points you need to cover. This prevents you from wandering off course, forgetting one of the questions you needed to ask, and having to place another call.

A good beginning: "I need to ask two or three questions. Do you have time to talk for a few minutes?" This tends to focus the mind of the person you are calling on your agenda and keeps the person from changing subjects after you have finished discussing one of the things you have called about.

After you have achieved the purpose of your call, you may want to ask, "Is there anything else we need to visit about before I let you go?" This courtesy signals the end of your agenda and is a simple way to terminate the call. If a person does have an item to discuss, the person will immediately mention it, rather than drifting into other areas.

That same question is useful for ending a conversation when someone else has called you and appears to be conducting a rambling conversation with no particular destination in mind.

One big taboo: Do not fail to return your calls—unless you want to intentionally disregard someone. Treat call-back requests with the same respect you would treat people in face-to-face conversations. Not calling people back is an insult. It signals to them that you view them and their needs as having low value.

32. *Good clock managers minimize the number and length of meetings.* Meetings are essential in business, churches, and organizations. Meetings per se are not time wasters. The way we manage meetings is the potential time waster.

Meetings accomplish one or more of four purposes:

A. Coordinate activities.
B. Exchange information.
C. Build morale.
D. Share decision making.

The following checklist can improve the quality of meetings:

- Decide whether we really need this meeting. Will it accomplish one or more of the four purposes listed above better than some other kind of communication?
- Send reminders of meeting times to each participant.
- Start on time and announce a stopping time at the beginning of the meeting.
- Distribute a written agenda at the beginning of the meeting, or in advance. An agenda can announce information, present relevant statistics, list options for action, and set the tone of the meeting through an inspiring quotation or story.

- Distribute all necessary written reports either in advance or at the meeting, depending on their length and complexity. Many participants will not read the reports in advance, but some will. This usually saves time because participants cannot legitimately delay making decisions by saying, "I have not had time to study this."
- Stay on the subject by saying, "That is an interesting idea. Maybe we need to study it some more so we can put it on the agenda for another time. But perhaps we ought to get back to the subject at hand."
- Refer complex issues to committees or individuals for research and ask them to bring recommendations to the next meeting.
- Put the meeting minutes in participants' hands within forty-eight hours after staff meetings. Send them by the next day's mail following church and organizational meetings.

Which of these tips can you use to help redeem the quality of your meetings?

33. *Good clock managers use their waiting time for reading, listening to cassette tapes, and reflection.* If you start using 60 minutes of dead time each day, you add 7 new hours a week, 30 new hours a month, and 365 new hours a year. That is enough time to write a book each year, read dozens of books, or accomplish innumerable important objectives. With audiotapes, you can easily transform the time you spend driving into continuing education. Are there other dead-time opportunities that you can bring to life?

34. *Good clock managers live balanced lives.* Using better time-management methods for the sole purpose of adding hours to your workweek is a dangerous and misdirected use of these methods. If you fill every hour with more work, you gradually eliminate the possibility of a normal lifestyle.

God's work is not done in your work alone—even if your work is professional church work. You also do God's work when you relate to your family. (This is another of the items that you and you alone can do.) This does not, of course, mean that your primary focus can be on leisure—especially if you are a high achiever. The critical factor is balance.

35. *Good clock managers reserve some time for planning how to manage their time.* "Nothing is easier than being busy and nothing more difficult than being effective," writes R. Alec Mackenzie. "The hardest

managerial work is thinking, an activity too often neglected by managers."[2]
Lack of planning time can arise from a number of causes:

- Some people find their planning time strangled by failure to delegate.
- Other leaders get intense emotional satisfaction from overcoming crises. If they become addicted to this excitement, they are not motivated to do the planning that could prevent such crises from recurring.
- Other leaders find more security in dealing with the huge piles on their desks than in taking the time to plan for improvements in their routines.
- Many leaders resist planning because it is such hard work. Most of us find it is more comfortable to cruise along in predictable routines. Yet the higher we move up in management, the more we must focus on the hard task of looking further ahead than we can clearly see.

A good time manager sets aside several hours every three months to plan, evaluate, and analyze how he or she and everyone in the organization use their time. Without that kind of planning, the organization finds itself constantly stressed by the tyranny of recurring, urgent crises that could be prevented.

36. *Good clock managers reserve time for spiritual reflection.* Our minds are the primary instruments God uses to play the song of his will in our lives. If we do not make time available for God to play his instrument, our work associates, our church, and our world will miss part of the music.

Jesus had the biggest job description God ever gave anyone—certainly bigger than yours and mine. Jesus left us the secret formula he used to accomplish his job: "My food is to do the will of him who sent me" (John 4:34). Jesus knew when to do what because he stayed in touch with an agenda other than his own.

At his winter home in Fort Myers, Florida, Thomas Edison planted several imported trees while he was trying to invent synthetic rubber. One of these trees is the Moreton Bay fig. Its roots run in every direction on top of the ground, but go only twelve inches deep into the soil—very poor protection against hurricanes. Leaders who stand tall over the long haul take time to grow deep spiritual roots. That procedure, which happens through prayer and meditation, is still an excellent time-management strategy.

How to Find Time

Leaders often lament their need to "find the time" to effectively accomplish one of their ministries. "Finding time" is a picturesque metaphor but a less than precise phrase. Time is never lost, only poorly used. If leaders see themselves as stewards of a precious gift and build on that perception with effective goals and habits, effective ministry results.

First, decide your life and ministry priorities. Second, decide to use your time to accomplish those priorities, instead of the dozens of other important matters that clamor for control of your clock.

Function from this life-management perspective, rather than a perspective of trying to use time more efficiently, and you will find the time about which other people only dream.

Jesus' Twenty Megatruths

How to Enter God's Kingdom

1. *You experience new ways of thinking and behavior when you enter God's kingdom.*

Being asked by the Pharisees when the kingdom of God was coming, [Jesus] answered them, "The kingdom of God is not coming with signs to be observed; nor will they say, 'Lo, here it is!' or 'There!' for behold, the kingdom of God is in the midst of you." (Luke 17:20-21)

Jesus answered him, "Truly, truly, I say to you, unless one is born anew, he cannot see the kingdom of God." (John 3:3)

What Helps You to Enter

2. *You enter God's kingdom only by a changed attitude of the heart, not by following a list of religious rules.*

"You hypocrites! Well did Isaiah prophesy of you, when he said:
    'This people honors me with their lips,
    but their heart is far from me;

in vain do they worship me,
teaching as doctrines the precepts of men.' " (Matt. 15:7-9)

In Luke 18:9-14, Jesus contrasts the phony righteousness of the Phari-
see who followed all the religious rules with the obvious virtue of the tax
collector who had followed no rules, but changed his heart.

3. *Concentrating on Christ strengthens your ability to enter and experience God's kingdom more fully.*

"I am the vine; you are the branches." (John 15:5*a*).

Again Jesus spoke to them, saying, "I am the light of the world; he who follows
me will not walk in darkness, but will have the light of life." (John 8:12).

4. *Prayer strengthens your ability to enter God's kingdom and experience it more fully.*

"Ask, and it will be given you; seek, and you will find; knock, and it will be
opened to you." (Matt. 7:7)

In Matthew 6:10, Jesus teaches his disciples to pray for the kingdom to
come.

What Restricts You from Entering

5. *You are blocked from entering God's kingdom unless you turn away
from self-centeredness.*

From that time Jesus began to preach, saying, "Repent, for the kingdom of
heaven is at hand." (Matt. 4:17)

In Matthew 7:13-14, Jesus' metaphor about the narrow gate teaches
that those who enter God's kingdom must make a clear choice between
two alternatives.

6. *Taking pride in your religious achievements makes it difficult to enter
God's kingdom.*

"Whoever humbles himself like this child, he is the greatest in the kingdom of heaven." (Matt. 18:4)

In Matthew 18:1-4, Jesus elaborates on the need for erasing religious pride in order to enter the kingdom.

7. *Financial wealth makes it more difficult for you to enter God's kingdom, because your money brings a false sense of power that distracts you from seeking something better.*

"It is easier for a camel to go through the eye of a needle than for a rich man to enter the kingdom of God." (Mark 10:25)

In Matthew 6:19-34, Jesus urges us to seek first God's kingdom rather than riches, since putting something else as first priority can block us from our relationship with God.

Rewards for Entering

8. *Though self-concern is not your goal, you receive rich rewards by entering God's kingdom.*

"Whoever loses his life for my sake and the gospel's will save it." (Mark 8:35*b*)

In Matthew 5:1-12, Jesus lists among the beatitudes numerous rewards for those who enter the kingdom.

9. *Entering God's kingdom gives you a sense of security that comes from believing your personal needs will be cared for.*

"But even the hairs of your head are all numbered. Fear not, therefore; you are of more value than many sparrows." (Matt. 10:30-31)

In Matthew 6:25-33, Jesus says that we should not be anxious about our need for food and clothing; God will care for us.

10. *Entering God's kingdom releases a new power in your life and thought processes that transcends the normal cause-and-effect patterns of your environment.*

"And whatever you ask in prayer, you will receive, if you have faith." (Matt. 21:22)

In Luke 9:1-6, Jesus sends the twelve disciples out with the power to heal the sick. In Luke 10:9 he instructs the seventy to heal the sick and informs them that the kingdom has come to them.

11. *Entering God's kingdom enables you to live joyfully.*

"These things I have spoken to you, that my joy may be in you, and that your joy may be full." (John 15:11)

"I came that they may have life, and have it abundantly." (John 10:10*b*)

12. *If you enter God's kingdom, you will continue to live in that consciousness beyond the time of physical death.*

"My sheep hear my voice, and I know them, and they follow me; and I give them eternal life, and they shall never perish, and no one shall snatch them out of my hand." (John 10:27-28)

Similar statements appear in Matthew 19:29; 25:46; Mark 10:30; Luke 18:30; John 3:15, 16; 4:14; 5:24; 6:27, 40, 47, 54; 10:28; 12:25; and 17:2-3.

By-products of Entering

13. *Entering God's kingdom gives you increased love and concern for other people.*

And he said to him, "You shall love the Lord your God with all your heart, and with all your soul, and with all your mind. This is the great and first commandment. And a second is like it, You shall love your neighbor as yourself." (Matt. 22:37-39)

In Luke 10:25-37, Jesus used the parable of the good Samaritan to connect loving God with the qualities of neighborliness and mercy, vividly asserting that loving God always involves an increased awareness of and concern for the needs of others.

14. *Entering God's kingdom makes you less judgmental about other people.*

"Judge not, that you be not judged." (Matt. 7:1)

In Matthew 13:24-30, Jesus illustrates the principle of leaving judgment to God instead of trying to do it ourselves.

15. *Entering God's kingdom gives you a more forgiving spirit.*

Then Peter came up and said to him, "Lord, how often shall my brother sin against me, and I forgive him? As many as seven times?" Jesus said to him, "I do not say to you seven times, but seventy times seven." (Matt. 18:21-22)

16. *Entering God's kingdom gives you the desire to help other people enter it, too.*

"Go therefore and make disciples of all nations, baptizing them in the name of the Father and of the Son and of the Holy Spirit, teaching them to observe all that I have commanded you." (Matt. 28:19-20*a*)

In Matthew 18:10-14, Jesus tells a parable about the urgent need to find one lost sheep, even though ninety-nine are safe in the fold.

17. *If you want to enter God's kingdom, you must live a self-giving life.*

"If any man would come after me, let him deny himself and take up his cross and follow me." (Matt. 16:24)

In Matthew 20:26-28, Jesus says that the person who wants to be greatest among his followers must be the servant of all the other servants.

Requirements for Continuing

18. *If your thinking and actions become self-centered, you can disconnect from God's kingdom.*

"Not every one who says to me, 'Lord, Lord,' shall enter the kingdom of heaven, but he who does the will of my Father who is in heaven." (Matt. 7:21)

In Matthew 7:15-27, Jesus illustrates the need for continued right attitudes and actions by saying that a tree is known by its fruits and by telling a story of two different kinds of house builders.

Negative Results of Not Entering

19. *Failing to enter God's kingdom brings you negative results.*

"So it will be at the close of the age. The angels will come out and separate the evil from the righteous, and throw them into the furnace of fire; there men will weep and gnash their teeth." (Matt. 13:49-50)

Future Manifestations of God's Kingdom

20. *God's kingdom will at an unspecified time become more fully and obviously manifested in the whole of creation.*

Jesus said to him, "You have said so. But I tell you, hereafter you will see the Son of man seated at the right hand of Power, and coming on the clouds of heaven." (Matt. 26:64)

In Matthew 24:3-44, Jesus talks extensively about an end time when the kingdom will become apparent and vividly real to all.

APPENDIX B

A SEVEN-PERSON FEEDBACK SYSTEM

I n one effective system for soliciting and hearing constructive feedback, the pastor or staff member selects seven persons he or she determines are personally supportive. Schedule a two-hour meeting with these seven persons for the purpose of completing the opinion poll below. Begin the session with prayer and with the request that everyone covenant together not to discuss the very personal issues and opinions you will cover in the meeting with anyone outside this group.

Ask the seven people *not* to sign their names on their completed opinion polls. Do not send the polls to them in the mail. Do not send the polls home with them, asking them to return them at another time. (This procedure may result in a couple of people phoning each other or others in the congregation. Such behavior encourages clusters of negative personalities to subvert a positive system into a negative head-hunting safari.) Ask the seven people not to discuss the items with one another while they are filling out their polls (this distorts the results). Above all, *do not give this opinion poll to the entire congregation on Sunday morning, by mail, or in any other manner.* This creates enormous distortion, because you are asking the opinions of people who do not know you well enough to have complete and accurate information. Then, too, giving these polls to the whole congregation creates among many persons the idea that something is wrong in the church. This is like scattering a handful of BBs in a shag carpet. It takes years to collect them all.

OPINION POLL

Most pastors and staff members have a high interest in self-improvement in their work and personal lives. Their calling drives them to desire a continual educational process regarding the ways others perceive them professionally and personally. Evaluation from peers is essential to that process.

The instrument that you have been invited to complete is not a test. Rather, it is an inventory of behaviors, attitudes, and skills that are usually a part of a church leader's life. Your role is to help the leader by completing the blanks in as honest a manner as you can. Do not be fearful of coming across as too critical. Valuable evaluation processes are built on honesty. Only in this way can the leader determine the points at which he or she needs to explore ways to strengthen a particular area of leadership.

Socrates said, "Know thyself." That is never totally possible when we work alone. Each of us sees only a portion of who he or she is. In working together with other caring persons, however, a larger picture emerges—one that can make us more effective servants of Christ and his church.

My Opinion Regarding the Abilities of _____
Please do not sign your name.

On a scale of 1 to 5, please rate _____'s abilities in the areas listed below, with 1 being the lowest value and 5 the highest value. If the item is not applicable in this person's ministry role, write "NA."

I. Preaching
  A. ____ clear
  B. ____ convincing
  C. ____ adequate in content
  D. ____ well organized
  E. ____ timely
  F. ____ spiritually uplifting
  G. ____ biblically based

II. Worship
A. ___ overall worship leadership style
B. ___ pastoral prayers
C. ___ children's sermons
D. ___ weddings
E. ___ funerals

III. Teaching
A. ___ children and youth
B. ___ adults
C. ___ membership classes for children
D. ___ membership classes for adults
E. ___ concerned about the congregation's total educational program
F. ___ well informed about the Bible
G. ___ aware of current community and world news

IV. Caring
A. ___ counseling
B. ___ visiting the sick
C. ___ visiting shut-ins
D. ___ concern for those who are grieving
E. ___ easy to talk with
F. ___ available when needed
G. ___ trustworthy with confidential matters

V. Evangelism
A. ___ inspires others to do the work of evangelism
B. ___ works hard personally at the task of evangelism each week
C. ___ trains others in evangelism work

VI. Organizational Management
A. ___ organizes people well
B. ___ is a prudent steward of the church's financial resources
C. ___ supervises paid staff effectively
D. ___ is a good administrator of the congregation's programs
E. ___ gives a sense of direction without dominating
F. ___ delegates satisfactorily

G. ___ leads in financial stewardship development

H. ___ recruits and trains others

VII. Community

A. ___ works well with other community churches

B. ___ works well with civic organizations

C. ___ is aware of community needs

VIII. Denomination

A. ___ encourages support for denominational work

B. ___ attends professional and denominational meetings

C. ___ is generally supportive of the denomination's basic beliefs

IX. Family

A. ___ spouse is supportive of ministry position (if married)

B. ___ home life is healthy

X. Outside Interests

A. ___ other interests and hobbies add positive balance to ministry role

B. ___ (if deriving income from other sources) other employment fits satisfactorily with ministry role

XI. Leadership

A. ___ is a hard worker

B. ___ is a good motivator

C. ___ is an effective spiritual leader

D. ___ is a source of inspiration

E. ___ exhibits personal enthusiasm

F. ___ supplies new ideas for programs

G. ___ promotes all church activities in an equal way

H. ___ is able to sense others' dissatisfaction

I. ___ promotes fun and fellowship

J. ___ seeks continuing education in ministry skills

K. ___ manages personal time and energy well

XII. Personal Traits

A. ___ gets along well with others

B. ___ is tactful
C. ___ cooperates
D. ___ listens well
E. ___ is flexible
F. ___ communicates ideas clearly
G. ___ is honest
H. ___ accepts criticism
I. ___ handles conflict effectively
J. ___ is comfortable in social conversations
K. ___ has a high energy level
L. ___ is neat in personal grooming
M. ___ dresses appropriately for various occasions
N. ___ shows sensitivity to the feelings of others
O. ___ is warm and approachable
P. ___ conveys an attitude of hopefulness
Q. ___ has spiritual depth
R. ___ is mentally healthy
S. ___ has a good sense of humor
T. ___ is temperate in consuming alcohol
U. ___ handles stress well
V. ___ speaks and writes with proper language usage
W. ___ has good posture
X. ___ has positive facial expressions
Y. ___ has high moral and ethical character
Z. ___ evidences personal devotional life

Collect the opinion polls and keep them in your possession. Go through the list and add up the totals for each item while the group takes a break. Put the totals on a clean inventory sheet. You may not agree with the totals, but in public life perception is reality. Even if the perception of these seven is inaccurate, you must deal with it as if it were accurate. Otherwise, it will deal with you in a far less pleasant way.

When the group gathers for the second part of the meeting, give each person a blank opinion poll, then ask everyone to write in the totals as you read them. (This is better than distributing a copy of the sheet on which you have written the totals, because it prevents people from losing touch with the discussion as their minds wander to the scores on other items.)

After giving the group the total scores, review each item, asking for comments on the explanations for extremely high scores and extremely low scores. (Hearing the positive feedback in conjunction with the negative feedback increases the possibility that you can receive insight in ways that produce constructive change.) As people share, firmly close your mouth, listen carefully, ask questions for clarification, and avoid defensive statements and excuses. Your willingness to listen increases their esteem for you and produces insights that you cannot obtain in any other manner.

If you desire, end the discussion session with some observations about continuing education options that you plan to pursue as a step toward improving your skills.

APPENDIX C

WHAT ARE YOUR SPIRITUAL GIFTABILITIES?

1. *Prophecy:* The giftability to receive and communicate a message from God to a particular audience with clarity and persuasive power. See Romans 12:6; 1 Corinthians 12:10, 28; Ephesians 4:11-14; Luke 7:26; Acts 15:32; Acts 21:9-11.
2. *Serving:* The giftability to identify and perform various details of work essential to the efficient functioning of the church. See Romans 12:7; 2 Timothy 1:16-18; Titus 3:14; Galatians 6:10; 1 Peter 4:10-11.
3. *Helping:* The giftability to help other Christians increase the effectiveness of their particular spiritual gifts. See 1 Corinthians 12:28; Romans 16:1-2; Acts 9:36; Luke 8:2-3; Mark 15:40-41.
4. *Teaching:* The giftability to communicate Christian information or concepts in ways that allow people to learn quickly and easily. See 1 Corinthians 12:28; Ephesians 4:11-14; Romans 12:7; Acts 18:24-28; 20:20-21.
5. *Encouraging:* The giftability to exhort, counsel, comfort, console, and encourage others in ways that strengthen their Christian faith commitment. See Romans 12:8; Hebrews 10:25; Acts 14:22.
6. *Giving:* The giftability to earn and give material resources to God's work liberally and cheerfully. See Romans 12:8; 2 Corinthians 9:2-8.
7. *Leadership:* The giftability to help Christians set goals congruent with God's will and to communicate these goals in ways that cause others to work voluntarily and harmoniously toward their achievement. See 1 Timothy 5:17; Hebrews 13:17.

8. *Mercy:* The giftability to feel empathy and compassion for those who suffer from mental, emotional, or physical hurts and to help them in ways that alleviate their suffering. See Romans 12:8; Mark 9:41; Luke 10:33-35; Acts 11:28-30.

9. *Pastor:* The giftability to assume long-term responsibility for the spiritual welfare of a Christian group. See Ephesians 4:11-14; Timothy 3:1-7; 1 Peter 5:1-3.

10. *Apostle:* The giftability to give leadership to a group of churches with a kind of spiritual authority that is spontaneously recognized by other people. See 1 Corinthians 12:28; Ephesians 4:11-14; Galatians 2:7-10.

11. *Missionary:* The giftability to minister effectively to people in another culture. See Acts 13:2-3; Acts 22:20-21; Romans 15:18-19.

12. *Evangelist:* The giftability to share the gospel of Christ with unbelievers in ways that encourage them to become active disciples and responsible members of his church. See Ephesians 4:11-14; 2 Timothy 4:5; Acts 8:5-6, 26-40; 21:8.

13. *Wisdom:* The giftability to see how a given item of knowledge applies to specific problems in the Body of Christ. See 1 Corinthians 2:6-13; 1 Corinthians 12:8; 2 Peter 3:15.

14. *Knowledge:* The giftability to find, collect, analyze, and clarify knowledge and then appropriately apply that information to problems in ways that promote the growth and well-being of the church. See 1 Corinthians 12:8; 2 Corinthians 11:6.

15. *Discernment of spirits:* The giftability to accurately judge character, recognize whether a person's behavior arises from godly or from evil motives, and see the difference between false teaching and divine truth in a confusing situation. See 1 Corinthians 12:10; 1 John 4:1-6.

16. *Healing:* The giftability to serve as the human instrument through whom God's healing power cures another person's physical or emotional need in ways different from those considered medically natural. See 1 Corinthians 12:9, 28; Acts 3:1-10; 5:12-16; 9:32-35; 28:7-10.

17. *Miracles:* The giftability to exercise faith in ways that observers perceive as altering the normal course of nature. See 1 Corinthians 12:10, 28; Acts 9:36-42; 19:11-20; 20:7-12; 2 Corinthians 12:12.

18. *Faith:* The giftability to clearly see the will and purpose of God and confidently act accordingly. See 1 Corinthians 12:9; Acts 11:22-24; 27:21-25.

19. *Administration:* The giftability to clearly understand the goals of a particular part of Christ's Body and to effectively execute designed plans for the accomplishment of these goals. See 1 Corinthians 12:28; Acts 6:1-7.

20. *Hospitality:* The giftability to enjoy providing a warm welcome to those who need food and lodging. See 1 Peter 4:9; Romans 12:13; 16:23; Acts 16:14-15; Hebrews 13:1-2.

21. *Instrumental music:* The giftability to play a musical instrument in ways that spiritually encourage and strengthen others. See 1 Samuel 16:14-23.

22. *Vocal music:* The giftability to spiritually strengthen people through singing. See Psalm 96:1-4.

23. *Writing:* The giftability to spiritually edify, instruct, and strengthen people with written words. See 1 John 2:1-28.

24. *Artistry:* The giftability to create, design, and build things that inspire others to greater faith and spiritual growth. See Exodus 31:1-11.

25. *Craftsmanship:* The giftability to construct or repair buildings or other items used to achieve God's purposes. See Exodus 31:3-5.

26. *Tongues:* The giftability to speak to God in unknown languages or to receive a message from God for his people through this medium. See 1 Corinthians 12:10, 28; 14:13-19; Acts 10:44-46; 19:1-6; Mark 16:17.

27. *Interpretation:* The giftability to translate the message of someone who speaks in unknown tongues. See 1 Corinthians 12:10, 30; 14:13, 26-28.

28. *Intercession:* The giftability to regularly pray for extended time periods and frequently see prayers answered to a degree much greater than that found among most Christians. See James 5:14-16; 1 Timothy 2:1-2; Colossians 1:9-12.

29. *Celibacy:* The giftability to enjoy remaining unmarried without suffering undue sexual temptation. See 1 Corinthians 7:7-8; Matthew 19:10-12.

30. *Martyrdom:* The giftability to undergo suffering for the faith to the point of death with a joyous and positive attitude. See Acts 7:54-60; Acts 12:1-5, 2 Corinthians 11:22-28.

NOTES

Chapter 3. Which Spiritual Food Energizes You?

1. Urban T. Holmes, III, *A History of Christian Spirituality: An Analytical Introduction* (Minneapolis: Seabury, 1980), pp. 3-7.
2. These four spiritual types are described in greater detail (along with a simple test that individuals can take to determine their spiritual type) in Corinne Ware's *Discover Your Spiritual Type* (Bethesda, Md.: The Alban Institute, 1995).
3. See William Strauss and Neil Howe, *Generations* (New York: William Morrow, 1991).
4. See Mike Regele, *Death of the Church* (Grand Rapids: Zondervan, 1995).

Chapter 4. Which Ministry Skills Have You Perfected?

1. David Sacks, "Spiritual Gifts," *Leadership,* summer 1992, p. 46.
2. Richard J. Leider and David A. Shapiro, *Repacking Your Bags* (San Francisco: Berrett-Koehler, 1995), p. 103.
3. Herb Miller, "How Do Pastors Learn?" *Net Results,* March 1995, pp. 19-20.
4. *Pastoral Leadership: Admired Values and Essential Skills Identified by United Methodist Laity,* prepared by The Office of Research, General Council on Ministries, The United Methodist Church, C. David Lundquist, general secretary (Dayton, Ohio, 1993), p. XII.
5. Herb Miller, "Clergy Self-Evaluation," *Net Results,* January 1990, pp. 5-8.
6. Two widely used spiritual gifts inventory tools are available in a *Net Results* reprint pac entitled *Creating a Positive Congregational Climate:* Carol Shanks, "Spiritual Gift Inventories: Closing the Information-Application Gap"; and Herb Miller, "How to Identify Your Spiritual Giftabilities." To order, call 806-762-8094.
7. A. W. Clausen, "The Challenge of Managing Change," *Executive Speeches,* August 1988, p. 5. Clausen is chairman and chief executive officer of Bank-America Corporation; his remarks were delivered at the Financial Executive Institute in Palo Alto, June 23, 1988.

Chapter 5. Which Leadership Traits Do You Possess?

1. See Daniel Goleman, *Emotional Intelligence* (New York: Bantam Books, 1995), p. XII.
2. Manfred F. R. Kets de Vries made this observation in his book *Life and Death in the Executive Fast Lane* (San Francisco: Jossey-Bass, 1995), p. 5. See Bernard Bass and Ralph Stogdill, *Bass and Stogdill's Handbook of Leadership*, rev. ed. (New York: Free Press, 1990).
3. Carl G. Jung, *Man and His Symbols* (New York: Dell, 1964), pp. 45-56.
4. Paul Dali, "The Entrepreneur: Soul of a Competitive America," *Executive Speeches*, March 1987, p. 16. Dali delivered his speech in Chicago, November 1986, at the High Tech Entrepreneur program.
5. John W. Gardner, *The Nature of Leadership* (Washington, D.C.: Independent Sector, 1986), pp. 25-26.
6. See Arthur Schlesinger, Jr., *The Chronicle of Higher Education*, May 28, 1986, p. 20.
7. Philip M. Albert, "PMA Picks," *PMA Advisor*, April 1987, p. 5.
8. "Managing to Be a Minister" (CRW Management Services), paper delivered by Drucker in 1971 at School of Theology, Claremont, Calif.
9. See Stewart Dinnen, "Column One," *The New Zealand Christian*, spring 1986.
10. Based on a list presented by Mike Mirarchi, Industrial Relations Manager of Frito-Lay, Inc., in remarks at the Masters Executive Training School, Texas Tech University, Arlington, Texas, January 19, 1987. Published in *Executive Speeches*, June 1987, p. 9.

Chapter 6. What Size Is Your Behavior?

1. Procedures for developing and operating care teams are available in the article entitled "Developing a Care Team," by Herb Miller in the *Net Results* reprint pac entitled *Strengthening Membership Care*, available from the *Net Results* Resource Center. To order, call 806-762-8094.
2. Colin L. Powell, *My American Journey* (New York: Random House, 1995), p. 261.
3. "Database," *U.S. News & World Report*, May 18, 1992, p. 12.
4. The following books are especially helpful to the leaders of churches in transition: Ronald Crandall, *Turnaround Strategies for the Small Church* (Nashville: Abingdon Press, 1995); Lyle E. Schaller, *The Middle-Sized Church* (1985), *Growing Plans* (1983), *The Seven-Day-a-Week Church* (1992), *Strategies for Change* (1993), all published in Nashville by Abingdon Press; John Ed Mathison, *Tried & True* (Nashville: Discipleship Resources, 1992); Leith Anderson, *A Church for the Twenty-First Century* (Minneapolis: Bethany House Publishers, 1992); Rick Warren, *The Purpose-Driven Church* (Grand Rapids, Mich.: Zondervan, 1995); Michael Slaughter, *Spiritual Entrepreneurs* (Nashville: Abingdon Press, 1995); William M. Easum, *Sacred Cows Make Gourmet Burgers* (Nashville: Abingdon Press, 1995).
5. John Ed Mathison, *Tried & True* (Nashville: Discipleship Resources, 1992), p. 107.

Chapter 7. What Shape Is Your Creativity?

1. F. Feitler and E. Tokar, "School Administration and Organizational Stress," *Journal of Educational Administration* 24, no. 2 (1986): pp. 254-71.

2. Kenneth H. Bastian, Jr., "Empowering Principal Leadership in Democratic Schools," (D.Ed. diss., Texas Tech University, May 1995).
3. M. J. O'Hair and D. O'Hair "A Model of Strategic Principal Communication During Performance Appraisal Interviews," *Journal of Research for School Executives* 2 (1991): pp. 13-22.
4. A. H. Eagley, S. J. Karau, and B. T. Johnson, "Gender and Leadership Style Among School Principals: A Meta-Analysis," *Educational Administration Quarterly* 28, no. 1 (1992): pp. 76-102.
5. C. Shakeshaft, I. Nowell, and A. Perry, "Gender and Supervision," *Theory Into Practice* 30, no. 2 (1991): pp. 137-38.
6. Joseph Campbell, with Bill Moyers, *The Power of Myth* (New York: Doubleday, 1988), p. 117.

Chapter 8. Does Your Personality Fit?

1. H. Newton Malony and Laura Fogwell Majovski, "The Role of Psychological Assessment in Predicting Ministerial Effectiveness," *Review of Religious Research* 28, no. 1 (September 1986): pp. 29-40.
2. Brian Jones, "7 Common Mistakes Church Planters Make Their 1st Year," *Visionary*, December 1995, pp. 5-6.
3. David Keirsey and Marilyn Bates, *Please Understand Me: Character & Temperament Types,* (Del Mar, Calif.: Gnosology Books, 1984), pp. 188-92.
4. William C. Cline, "Type and Effective Church Planting," Proceedings: Psychological Type and Culture-East West, Second Multicultural Research Symposium, January 5-7, 1996, University of Hawaii, Manoa.
5. Eugene Roehlkepartain, "Effective Pastors," *Christian Ministry*, March/April 1992, p. 7.
6. Tom Parker, *In One Day* (Boston: Houghton Mifflin, 1984), p. 63.
7. Neil Backham, Lawrence Friedman, Richard Ruff, *Getting Partnering Right* (New York: McGraw-Hill, 1996), p. 11.
8. See *Net Results* (March 1981), p. 3, summarizing research by Speed B. Leas, *How to Deal Constructively With Clergy-Lay Conflict* (Bethesda, Md.: The Alban Institute, 1980).
9. Albert C. Outler, *Evangelism and Theology in the Wesleyan Spirit* (Nashville: Discipleship Resources, 1996), pp. 18, 28.
10. James L. Lowery, Jr., *Enablement Information Service Newsletter,* January 1987, p. 2, quoting from *The Midwest Career Development Newsletter,* January 1987.

Chapter 9. What Is Your Style?

1. See David McClelland, in Richard J. Kirk, "What Motivates You: Achievement, Affiliation, or Power?" *Action Information* (The Alban Institute, Bethesda, Md.), September 1979, pp. 8-9.
2. James M. Kouzes and Barry Z. Posner, *Credibility* (San Francisco: Josey-Bass, 1993), p. 20.
3. Melanie K. Onnen, "The Relationship of Clergy Leadership Characteristics to Growing or Declining Churches" (D.Ed. diss., University of Louisville, 1987), p. iv.
4. See Bernard M. Bass, *Leadership and Performance Beyond Expectations* (New York: Free Press, 1985).

5. Fred Craddock, *Sermons Preached at the Altar,* audiocassette (St. Louis: Chalice Press, 1990).
6. Colin L. Powell, *My American Journey* (New York: Random House, 1995), p. 613.
7. Mark A. Taylor, "From the Editor," *The Lookout,* October 5, 1986, p. 8.

Chapter 10. Do Your Clock Habits Achieve Your Goals?

1. R. Alec Mackenzie, *The Time Trap* (New York: McGraw-Hill, 1972), pp. 3-4.
2. Ibid., p. 38.